BARBECUE
&
GRILL

STÉPHANE REYNAUD'S

BARBECUE
&
GRILL

PHOTOGRAPHY BY MARIE-PIERRE MOREL
ILLUSTRATIONS BY JOSÉ REIS DE MATOS

LYONS PRESS
Guilford, Connecticut
An imprint of Globe Pequot Press

ODE TO THE BARBECUE

The time has come when the sun scorches like embers red with desire, the time has come when the kitchen calls us outside, the time has come to barbecue. The toes have found their cruising speed—spreadout; the body has found its favorite position—stretched out; and the head its preferred state—empty. Spring lays its cards on the table. We want to live outside, we want to eat outside, we want to cook outside. No more gurgling casseroles and misted window panes. The table calls for friends to be gathered around it, the ice cubes tinkle madly, the forecast is fine! You lift up the dust-covered tarp in the backyard, move aside the three bikes, still spattered with mud, so that you can finally reach the must-have accessory of the moment: the BARBECUE. You hasten to clean the grill discreetly, away from prying eyes, the culinary vestiges from the previous year still being clear and present. You empty out what's left of the ashes and a few rusty beer bottle caps jog your memory. You rub the outside of the barbecue with a damp cloth to bring back some sheen to your grilling companion. It's beautiful, almost like new, ready to throw your future guests into a panic with its benevolent plumes of smoke—because the barbecue has the inexplicable peculiarity of always sighing over that day's assembled guests, whatever the direction of the wind. It clings to the little clothing you're wearing, imprinting its smell upon them, and gets under your skin!

ODE TO THE
BAR
BE
CUE

TABLE OF CONTENTS

WHAT TO CHOOSE?

Choosing a barbecue can sometimes be like a Chinese puzzle: electric, gas, wood, with hot plate, rotisserie… What to choose? It's essential first of all to picture the site where your future culinary jousts will take place, so that you can secure the perimeter. This is not the place to cut corners—we don't want to send the neighborhood up in flames! A barbecue needs to be in an isolated spot without too much vegetation around it, and preferably close to a source of water.

THE ELECTRIC BARBECUE

Often small in size, the electric barbecue has a home on accommodating balconies. It is generally not high-powered and doesn't give a good sear to items like beef rib roasts. On the other hand, it fosters good neighborly relations in virtue of its being practically smokeless. A water trough under the elements catches grease and prevents it catching alight: the sausages give thanks, the sardines let out a phew of relief! It is perfect for the food-loving couple and is easily transportable. Second, third, fourth floor, long live the electric barbecue!

THE GAS BARBECUE

The gas barbecue has earned its stripes in the eyes of lovers of all forms of grilling. Warning: when bringing the barbecue out of hibernation, it is essential to check the hose connecting the gas cylinder to the barbecue. Rub the connections with soapy water. If any bubbles appear: STOP. You need to change the hose. If the flame is small and yellow, it might be that your gas jets are blocked; turn everything off and wash with lots of water. Once these precautions have been taken, a gas barbecue is easy to use: you light a spark, open up the gas, and away you go. Gas barbecues sometime contain volcanic rocks that are heated by the gas and distribute the heat evenly. They let you sear foods well while managing the heat easily. Gas barbecues are often the most complete in terms of accessories—a cover to create an oven with a temperature control, rotisserie, smoke box, side gas burner, adjustable hot plate…

THE WOOD-FIRED BARBECUE

The wood-fired barbecue is undoubtedly the one most prized by connoisseurs for the superb flavor it gives to food. Its use requires much more thoughtful management, the embers don't happen in the blink of an eye and controlling the temperature and flames can also present a handicap. We all have a memory of sausages that were simultaneously burnt and not cooked, singed and bitter from a fat fire… But we also all have the memory of the beef rib cutlet that was perfectly caramelized on the outside and juicy inside, determined to convert the most vegetarian of vegetarians. The wood-fired barbecue offers the luxury of choosing between a multitude of fuels—pine cones, vine shoots, pine needles, tree wood (yes, it exists!)— according to what's being cooked (ask my friend, he will tell you that duck breasts can only be cooked over vine shoots lit with the sports pages of a newspaper). A wood-fired barbecue nevertheless presents environmental hazards: a gust of wind, a flying ember, and 10 acres go up in smoke!

THE BARBECUE HOT PLATE

The barbecue hot plate is the first cousin of the barbecue grill. It allows for almost the same cooking styles as the grill, with the exception of that much sought-after touch of smokiness and char.

The major advantage of the hot plate is that it offers the possibility of cooking several items at the same time with only a little fat—get thee behind me, cholesterol! You take a recipe, combine the ingredients and cook everything together. Sauces and marinades can be added directly without disappearing through a barbecue grill. A hot plate can be bought as a stand-alone appliance or as a barbecue attachment. Like barbecues, both electric and gas hot plates are available. The most important thing is to check how much power the hot plate has so that you can get a good sear on the food. It needs to heat to at least 500°F, or else forget it!

The coating is also something to consider when choosing your hot plate. Stainless steel is easy to maintain but offers less heat transfer than cast-iron, which is not as easy to maintain. After each use, rub the plate while it's still hot with vinegar and water (this will remove the food tastes) using a metal scraper. Then apply a thin coat of oil (this will prevent the oxidization of cast-iron hot plates).

IDEAL FOR
ONIONS
SQUID
MUSHROOMS
TOMATOES
CHOPPED VEGETABLES
MARINADES

GEAR

When you're talking barbecue, you're talking special equipment. The barbecue specialist does not tolerate amateurism.

- A longer fork, used to avoid a depilatory episode giving you an arm like a Tour de France cyclist. It is made from rigid steel in order to stand up to the 4 lb beef rib cutlet.
- A pair of tongs of substantial length, for easy turning of tumultuous sausages.
- A steel brush, for scrubbing the grill while it still glows with shame.
- An appropriate small stainless-steel case, for holding all the essentials, like an overnight bag full of make-up, which will consolidate your status as a pro. It's good for showing off and would be a great present for your birthday.

Now you're equipped to grill, brown and sear! The only thing left is to slip on the 'Daddy's a Chef' apron you got on Father's Day, make sure the ice-cube trays are full to overflowing (don't forget to check how much wood or charcoal you have if your barbecue is wood-fired), and slip on your favorite hat.
The embers are smoking, the skewers are marinating, the guests are pouring in…It's cooking as an artform!

MAINTENANCE

The maintenance of the barbecue is as important as the foundation of your relationship, like the cement that holds everything together.
A barbecue party often begins with a sudden awakening: the weather's fine, quick, let's have a barbecue. There's a bustle over the morning coffee, phone calls are made, invitations are sent out, let's eat! Your partner is already busy trying to scour the grill—put away like the last time—with broad strokes of the metal brush in a bubble bath (a mix of soap and vinegar). Meanwhile you ponder.
Your partner jumps in the car to stock a refrigerator that has too much empty space for the expected crowd. You check that the beer is in the fridge. Your partner prepares the salad, sets the table. You try to light the briquettes or get the gas ignited: 'Can you give me a hand? I can't get it to work!'
The guests have arrived, your partner gives the barbecue grill—now hot—another rub, and serves drinks. You drink.
Your partner gives you a nudge: 'You should put the meat on to cook.' You sigh and comply. Your partner checks if the meat is cooked, serves the meat, you savor the results: 'You have to admit, barbecuing is such a social way of eating, and it gives you a rest from the cooking as well.' Your partner clears the table, puts things away, makes the coffee, you bring out more wine. The barbecue will stay outside, flecked with the remains of the day's meal…You don't have the strength to put it away: 'I'm too worn out from cooking all day, I'm going to watch the afternoon game on TV.'

BUILDING A BARBECUE

The fantasy of cooking just anywhere, around a flame, as night falls on a steamy day, the heat of the moment like the thrill of a wedding night, lives inside all of us. We picture ourselves with a stack of wood, a hand-caught trout, a few vegetables gleaned from an abandoned field, a bottle of good red wine at the bottom of the backpack, the wide open spaces, a touch of MacGyver, a Swiss knife in the pocket…

Survivor only exists on television. Saturday adventurers must above all observe very strict rules of safety to avoid the firefighters being called out again. The site needs to be suitable for improvizing a barbecue, and during summer in many areas such activities are strictly forbidden. The weather musn't be too dry, there mustn't be any wind, and the area must be completely cleared.

That day's 'Boston Rob' must first of all dig an 8 x 8 inch trench marking out the area of the barbecue, with rocks arranged in the center along the trench. The fire must be small, using dry wood.

The trout is cooked old-style, speared like a marshmallow on some green wood, and above all you make sure that the embers are TOTALLY extinguished when you leave to rejoin civilization. Only then can you say that you've won *Survivor*.

BASTING

Items that need to be cooked for a longer time mustn't dry out from exposure to the prolonged heat of a good set of embers—you need to baste them while cooking. To add flavor to chicken, lamb and roasts, use a bunch of aromatic herbs dipped in olive oil or the marinade of the hour. These herbs need to have some resistance, so it is better to use your choice—or a mixture—of herbs, such as thyme, rosemary, bay leaves, sage…Tie them all together with string, dip the bunch in oil and generously caress the beast so it gives the best of itself.

SALT RUBS

Meat and fish often need special attention before a hot night out. They like being taken care of before getting into the action. Pamper them like your sweetheart on date night, bath salts become massage salts—rub them in to bring out their full intensity. The meat and fish are in for a serious relaxation session for a successful gourmet rendezvous.

SICHUAN SALT

2 tablespoons sea salt
1 tablespoon sichuan peppercorns
1 tablespoon superfine sugar

Pound everything together roughly in a mortar and pestle. This is a good seasoning for fish. The freshness of the pepper paired with the sugar makes it a rub that's both sharp and sweet.

PROVENÇAL SALT

2 tablespoons sea salt
1 teaspoon dried rosemary
1 tablespoon dried thyme
1 teaspoon ground cardamom

Pound everything together roughly in a mortar and pestle. This one accentuates the flavor of meat and fish and brightens a still-grey sky with the sunshine of cardamom.

CURRY SALT

1 teaspoon curry powder
1 teaspoon fennel seeds
1 teaspoon ground ginger
1 teaspoon coriander seeds
20 cloves
1 dried bird's eye chili
2 tablespoons sea salt

Pound the spices in a mortar and pestle before combining them with the salt.
Your dishes will come to life with the spices of India.
Lamb and chicken dance in a sari.

SPICY SALT

4 bird's eye chilis
1 teaspoon black peppercorns
1 teaspoon dried parsley
1 teaspoon cumin
2 tablespoons sea salt

Pound the spices in a mortar and pestle before combining them with the salt.
To be used in moderation. A salt that lights your fire…
Use with both meats and fish.

BARBECUE SAUCE AND ITS VARIATIONS

Barbecuing naturally lends a quite distinctive taste to foods. The incomparable aroma of a bunch of vine shoots will take duck breast to another level, the resinous note of pine cones adds freshness to fish, and so on.

We can obviously be content going no further than these small culinary 'bonuses' in our fiery epics, but the barbecue chef will want more, and this is the person we need to make happy, to satisfy, to please.

Sauces and marinades then become the signature of the dish, they elevate it to the pantheon of a collective 'mmmm' and give a personal touch to the flavor of the day. Some meats need to excite our desire before being consumed. They need to tenderize, rest, lounge about in a suitable marinade.

The sensual minglings of such a bath are rediscovered on the plate. The flavors blended beforehand are tattooed onto the heart of the meat when it is cooked. The dish of the day can then be eaten as is, rough and ready, or sauced at leisure after cooking, to smooth over the encounter. Other dishes require a friendly jolt to reveal their full potential, and in these cases the sauce plays the role of detonator. When served with grilled foods, it should take them to the next level without distorting their essence.

The cooked product comes first, the sauce becomes its ally and should also exist in perfect harmony with the dish's accompaniments so as not to run into an unfortunate marriage on the plate.

MAYONNAISE AND ITS VARIATIONS

BASIC

¾ cup mild vegetable or sunflower oil
1 whole egg
1 tablespoon dijon mustard
1 tablespoon vinegar
salt and pepper

Place all the ingredients in the bowl of a food processor.
Process until you obtain the desired consistency.

COCKTAIL

To the basic recipe, add 1 tablespoon ketchup and
1 teaspoon of cognac.

WHOLEGRAIN MUSTARD

In the basic recipe, replace the traditional mustard with
2 tablespoons wholegrain mustard, add 2 tablespoons olive oil.

GARLIC

To the basic recipe, add 2 garlic cloves, 1 tablespoon olive oil
and 2 tablespoons créme fraiche or Greek yogurt.

HERB

To the basic recipe, add 1 bunch chives, finely snipped,
2 sprigs tarragon, finely chopped and 1 French shallot,
finely chopped.

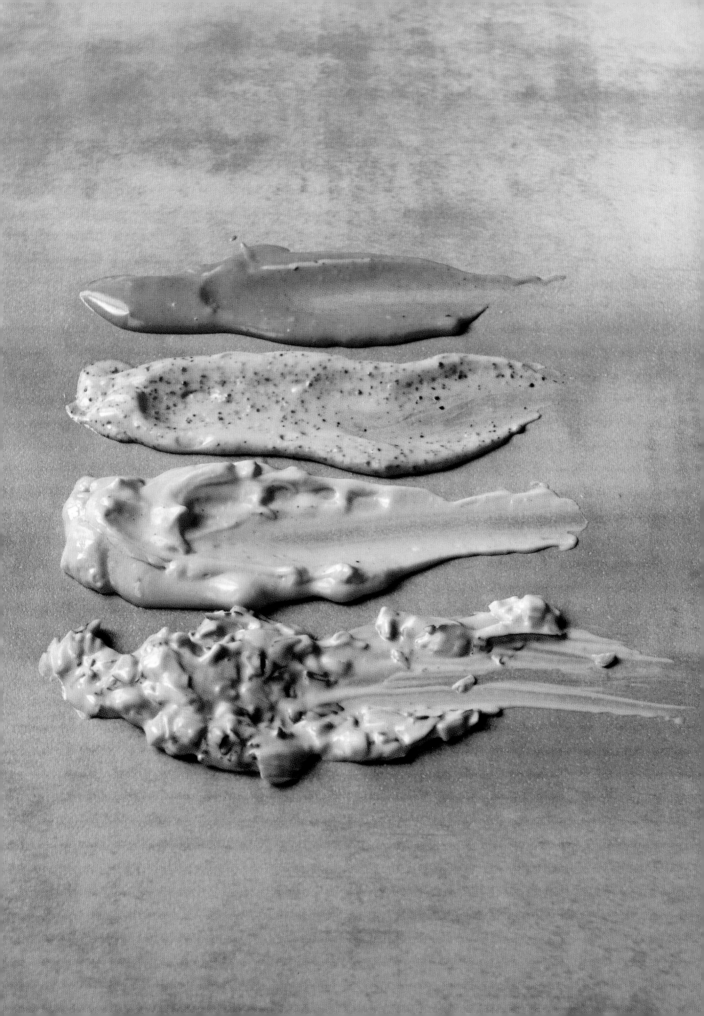

EMULSION SAUCES

These classics are not made often enough, unfortunately, for fear of finding oneself with a split sauce that will then have to face the snickers of guests. Nevertheless, it's a pleasure to enjoy a juicy rare beef rib cutlet generously coated with béarnaise sauce, and a joy to savor a grilled fish covered in beurre blanc…Jump in, tuck in, you're welcome.

BEURRE BLANC

7 oz butter
3 egg yolks
juice of half a lemon
salt and pepper

Melt the butter in a saucepan, keep it at room temperature. Whisk the egg yolks in the top part of a double boiler with 3 tablespoons of cold water, until the mixture is pale and thick. (Important: the temperature mustn't go over 176°F to prevent cooking the yolks.) Whisking continuously, gradually add the melted butter (discarding any liquid that has separated out), then the lemon juice and season.

HOLLANDAISE

8 oz butter
1 French shallot
½ cup dry white wine
2 teaspoons white wine vinegar
4 egg yolks
salt and pepper

Melt the butter in a saucepan, keep it at room temperature. Peel and finely chop the French shallot.
Over medium heat, soften the French shallot in the white wine and vinegar, then allow to reduce until almost dry. Off the heat, add the egg yolks, whisking in the top part of a double boiler until the mixture becomes pale and thick. (Important: the temperature mustn't go over 176°F to prevent cooking the yolks.) Whisking continuously, gradually add the melted butter (discarding any liquid that has separated out), and season.

BÉARNAISE

9 oz butter
2 French shallots
½ bunch tarragon
½ bunch chervil
3 tablespoons dry white wine
2 tablespoons white wine vinegar
1 teaspoon coarsely ground black pepper
4 egg yolks
salt

Melt the butter in a saucepan, keep it at room temperature. Peel and finely chop the French shallots, chop the herbs. Over medium heat, soften the French shallots in the white wine and vinegar, add the herbs and the pepper then allow to reduce until almost dry. Off the heat, add the egg yolks, whisking them in the top of a double boiler until the mixture becomes pale and thick. (Important: the temperature mustn't go over 176°F to prevent cooking the yolks.) Whisking continuously, gradually add the melted butter (discarding any liquid that has separated out), and season.

CREAMY SAUCES

Creamy sauces are always a hit with the guests of the day. Their smoothness, indulgence and generosity delight impatient tastebuds. They are a blue-chip, minimum-risk investment for a satisfied table.

PEPPER

1 French shallot
1 tablespoon coarsely ground black pepper
3 tablespoons cognac
¾ cup veal stock
¾ cup cream
salt

Peel and finely chop the French shallot. Toast the pepper in a dry saucepan, flambé with the cognac, add the French shallot, and veal stock, reduce for 5 minutes. Add the cream, reduce until it reaches the desired consistency, then season.

SORREL

1 French shallot
½ cup white wine
¾ cup fish stock
¾ cup cream
1 bunch sorrel
salt and pepper

Peel and finely chop the French shallot. Put the white wine with the French shallot in a saucepan, reduce until almost dry, add the fish stock and the cream, reduce until it reaches the desired consistency. Finely chop the sorrel, add it to the sauce, cook for 5 minutes then season.

ROQUEFORT

5½ oz roquefort cheese
1¼ cups cream

Melt the roquefort cheese in the cream. Reduce until it reaches the desired consistency.

SAFFRON

1 garlic clove
1 tablespoon pastis (aniseed flavored liqueur)
¾ cup fish stock
¾ cup cream
1 pinch of saffron
1 tablespoon poppy seeds
salt and pepper

Peel and finely chop the garlic. Put the pastis and garlic in a saucepan, reduce until almost dry. Add the fish stock, cream and saffron, reduce until it reaches the desired consistency. Add the poppy seeds before serving and season.

CHAPTER I

28
SKEWERS

SK
EW
ERS

DIY SKEWERS

When you're talking barbecue, you're talking skewers, the one is unthinkable without the other. The skewer refers both to the skewer that the foods—meat, fish, crustaceans, fruit—are threaded onto, whether metal or wood…and the food cooked this way! Skewers can be a one-dish meal by alternating vegetables with meat and fish. When dealing with fragile foods, it is essential to push the items close together so they don't disappear when you come to cooking them, swallowed up by hungry embers.

Metal skewers are the preferred choice for more lengthy cooking; they will stand up to the heat. Be careful not to put them directly in your mouth or it's a guaranteed burn. Single-use wooden or bamboo skewers are used for shorter cooking times. To help them stand up to the heat better, soak wooden and bamboo skewers in salted water for 10 minutes before using them.

You can also make your own skewers by using aromatic stems from plants such as lemongrass, rosemary, and licorice. The skewer will then give a distinctive taste to the dish by diffusing its own flavor through the food.

SKEWERS

HONEY PORK

With your partner, the sweet tooth

Serves 6
Preparation time 20 minutes
Cooking time 10 minutes over gentle heat

1 lb 9 oz pork fillet
2 small, firm zucchinis
Marinade:
3 tablespoons liquid honey
⅔ cup white port (or dry sherry)
1 teaspoon ground ginger
2 tablespoons sesame seeds
salt and pepper

Cut the pork into 1¼ inch cubes. Cut the zucchini
into rounds.
For the marinade, combine the honey with the port, ginger
and sesame seeds, season.
Assemble the skewers, alternating the pork with the zucchini
(packed close together). Coat generously with marinade.
Cook over a gentle heat for about 10 minutes, dipping
regularly in the marinade.

Drink with: fruity white with muscat undertones

PORK WITH DRIED FRUIT

With anyone it reminds you of

Serves 6
Preparation time 10 minutes
Cooking time 10 minutes over gentle heat

1 lb 9 oz pork fillet
6 dried figs
12 pitted prunes
12 dried apricots
⅔ cup olive oil
1 tablespoon herbes de Provençe (usually marjoram,
  oregano, rosemary, thyme)
salt and pepper

Cut the pork into 1¼ inch cubes. Halve the dried figs and
remove the stems. Assemble the skewers, alternating meat and
dried fruit. Drizzle with some olive oil, scatter over the herbes
de Provençe, season.
Cook over gentle heat for 10 minutes. Be careful not to burn
the dried fruit.

**Drink with: white with lots of oak on the nose and a hint
of apricot**

VEAL FILLET WITH STREAKY SPECK

With the in-laws (always needing a good feed)

Serves 6
Preparation time 20 minutes
Marinating time 3 hours
Cooking time 10 minutes over gentle heat

1 lb 9 oz veal schnitzels
12 thin slices speck (smoked bacon or ham), cartilage removed
Marinade:
⅔ cup sesame oil
½ cup whisky
1 teaspoon ground bay
1 tablespoon coarsely ground black pepper

Slice the veal into 12 strips the same size as the slices of speck
(thin and all the same width). Arrange them in a dish.
For the marinade, combine the sesame oil with the whisky,
ground bay and pepper, cover the veal with this mixture.
Cover with plastic wrap and chill for 3 hours.
Place a slice of veal on a slice of speck and twist them.
Thread each twist on a skewer and cook over a gentle barbecue
heat for 10 minutes. Since the bacon is already salty, there is no
need to add salt.

Drink with: your in-laws of course!

BEEF WITH FIGS AND SAKE

With friends who've just come back from Japan

Serves 6
Preparation time 20 minutes
Cooking time 8 minutes over high heat

1 lb 5 oz rump steak
¾ cup sake
1 teaspoon ground ginger
6 fresh figs
5½ oz speck (smoked bacon or ham)
12 bulb spring onions
salt and pepper

Cut the rump steak into square pieces ¼ inch thick. Combine with the sake and ginger. Cut the figs and the speck into slices of the same thickness, cut the bulb spring onions in two. Make up the skewers, starting with half a bulb spring onion, then alternate beef, fig and speck. Finish with another half a bulb spring onion. Grill over high heat for 8 minutes, turning the skewer regularly, then season.

Drink with: the sake your friends brought back for you

STEAK WITH SHISO

With my cousins, being sometimes a little shiso

Serves 6
Preparation time 10 minutes
Cooking time 7–8 minutes over high heat

1 lb 12 oz skirt steak
assorted baby shiso leaves (purple mint/perilla)
salt and pepper
Marinade:
1 garlic clove
¾ cup port
½ cup balsamic vinegar
1 tablespoon fresh thyme, chopped finely
2 tablespoons olive oil

Cut the steak into cubes. For the marinade, peel and crush the garlic. Combine the port with the vinegar, add the garlic and thyme, bring to the boil. Reduce by half then add the olive oil. Reserve a little marinade for serving.
Place the steak cubes in the marinade, then thread them on the skewers. Cook 7–8 minutes over high heat depending on how you like your meat cooked, season. Serve scattered with baby shiso and drizzle over a little reserved marinade.

Drink with: powerful and rich Pinot Noir

BEEF AND PRAWNS

With one who prefers fish and another who prefers meat, so they may be reconciled

Serves 6
Preparation time 20 minutes
Marinating time 3 hours
Cooking time 7–8 minutes over high heat

1 lb 5 oz rump steak
18 jumbo shrimp
Marinade:
2 garlic cloves
1 tablespoon ketchup
3 tablespoons concentrated meat extract
1 tablespoon olive oil
1 teaspoon coarsely ground black pepper

Cut the rump steak into square slices, ¼ inch thick.
For the marinade, peel the garlic and chop it finely. Combine the garlic with the ketchup, meat extract, olive oil and pepper. Place the steak in the marinade and chill for 3 hours. Cut the shrimp in two. Assemble the skewers, alternating shrimp and beef, and cook them over high heat for 7–8 minutes.

Drink with: a winemaker you know

MEATBALLS WITH CILANTRO

With a golfer who has lost his ball

Serves 6
Preparation time 30 minutes
Cooking time 5 minutes over high heat

1 bunch cilantro
1 lemongrass stem
2 French shallots
1 garlic clove
2 large Melba toasts
1 lb 12 oz ground beef
2 eggs
salt and pepper

Finely chop the cilantro and lemongrass. Peel and finely chop the French shallots and garlic clove. Crush the Melba toasts to crumbs. Combine the ground beef with the eggs, then add all the other ingredients, season. Roll the meatballs in the palm of your hands to the size of a large ball (approx 1¼ inch diameter). Cook the meatballs over high heat according to how you like your meat cooked.

Drink with: anything aniseed-flavored, of course!!

BEEF WITH APPLES AND SPICES

With pals from the office

Serves 6
Preparation time 5 minutes
Cooking time 10 minutes over high heat

1 lb 5 oz rump steak
2 granny smith apples
Marinade:
1 garlic clove
1 orange
1 teaspoon liquid honey
1 pinch ground cinnamon
1 pinch ground cardamom
1 pinch ground chili
3 tablespoons soy sauce
1 tablespoon Maggi seasoning sauce

Cut the rump steak into square slices ¼ inch thick.
For the marinade, peel the garlic and chop it finely. Zest and juice the orange, combine with the honey, spices, soy sauce and Maggi sauce. Reserve some marinade for serving.
Dip the meat in the remaining marinade. Halve the apples, remove the seeds, cut each half into slices the same size as the meat. Thread the meat and apple slices on skewers, grill over high heat for 5 minutes. Serve coated with the reserved marinade.

Drink with: rich red filled with the aroma of smoke and the smell of truffle

ONGLET KEBABS

With a real carnivore

Serves 6
Preparation time 15 minutes
Cooking time 5 to 10 minutes over high heat

1 lb 12 oz onglet (hanger/flank steak)
1 smoked duck breast
12 bulb spring onions
24 cherry tomatoes
24 button mushrooms
salt
Chili oil:
½ cup olive oil
1 teaspoon ground piment d'Espelette (or hot paprika)
1 teaspoon sesame seeds
1 teaspoon coarsely ground black pepper

Cut the steak into 1¼ inch cubes. Remove the fat from the smoked duck breast, slice into ¼ inch thick strips, then into small rectangles. Halve the bulb spring onions. For the chili oil, combine the olive oil with the chili, sesame seeds and pepper.
On a skewer, thread half a bulb spring onion, then alternate meat, duck, tomato, mushroom and finish with another half a bulb spring onion. Cook the skewers over high heat for 5–10 minutes, according to how you like your meat cooked. Drizzle with chili oil, season with salt.

Drink with: gutsy quaffing red

44
SKEWERS

GARLIC AND CHILI CHICKEN

With a fire-breather

Serves 6
Preparation time 20 minutes
Cooking time 15 minutes over gentle heat

½ cup tamarind sauce
1 tablespoon brown sugar
6 free-range chicken breast fillets
6 garlic cloves
3 mild long green chilies
3 mild long red chilies
1 small bird's eye chili
salt and pepper

Heat the tamarind sauce with the brown sugar. Cut the chicken breasts in three lengthways. Peel and finely chop the garlic. Finely chop the mild red and green chilies as well as the bird's eye chili. Combine the garlic and chilies. Dip the pieces of chicken breast in the tamarind sauce, thread them on skewers and roll them in the chili-garlic mixture, pressing it on firmly. Cook the skewers over gentle heat for about 15 minutes, season.

Drink with: cherry-flavored powerful rosé

PINEAPPLE CHICKEN

With your favorite Caribbean music

Serves 6
Preparation time 20 minutes
Marinating time 24 hours
Cooking time 15 minutes over gentle heat

6 free-range chicken breast fillets
1¼ cups coconut cream
1 pinch ground chili
1 lime
1 ripe pineapple
salt and pepper

Cut the chicken breasts into cubes and place them in the coconut cream with the chili powder and the zest and juice of the lime. Cover and chill this mixture for 24 hours. Peel the pineapple, remove the 'eyes', cut it into quarters then into pieces the same size as the pieces of chicken. Thread the chicken and the pineapple onto the skewers. Cook over gentle heat for about 15 minutes. Season.

Drink with: icy-cold pineapple punch

BOLLYWOOD

With a student of Asian languages

Serves 6
Preparation time 20 minutes
Marinating time 24 hours
Cooking time 15 minutes over gentle heat

6 free-range chicken breast fillets
Marinade:
2 garlic cloves
1¾ oz fresh ginger
½ bunch cilantro, finely chopped
1 teaspoon ground cumin
½ teaspoon ground turmeric
1 pinch cayenne pepper
1 pinch grated nutmeg
2 small tubs plain yogurt
1 tablespoon sunflower oil
juice of 1 lemon
½ teaspoon superfine sugar
1 tablespoon ketchup
salt

Cut the chicken breasts into cubes.
For the marinade, peel and finely chop the garlic and ginger. In a mortar and pestle, pound the garlic and ginger to a paste with the coriander, cumin, turmeric, cayenne pepper and nutmeg. Combine this mixture with the yogurt, add the oil, lemon juice, sugar and ketchup, season.
Place the chicken in the marinade, cover and chill for 24 hours. Reserve some marinade for cooking. Thread the chicken onto the skewers. Cook over gentle heat for about 15 minutes. Don't hesitate to add some of the reserved marinade while cooking.

Drink with: dry full-bodied chardonnay

MASSAMAN LAMB

With a loudmouth, to spice up his rants

Serves 6
Preparation time 15 minutes
Cooking time 10 minutes over high heat

1 lb 12 oz lamb leg meat
fresh ginger, to serve (optional)
1 teaspoon coriander seeds
1 teaspoon whole cumin seeds
1 teaspoon ground cinnamon
20 cloves
5 dried red chilies
Massaman sauce:
3 garlic cloves, finely chopped
1 French shallot, finely chopped
¼ oz fresh ginger, finely chopped
zest of 1 lime
1 teaspoon shrimp paste
oil
1 cup coconut milk

Cut the lamb leg into 1¼ inch cubes. Thread these
onto skewers, with a round of fresh ginger on one end, if
desired. In a non-stick frying pan, toast the spices with the
chilies and grind them in a mortar and pestle. Sprinkle these
spices over the skewers.
For the massaman sauce, place the garlic, French shallot,
ginger, kaffir lime zest and shrimp paste in the mortar and
pestle and pound until you have a smooth paste. Sauté
1 tablespoon of this mixture in a little oil (keep the rest of
the paste for another recipe, it will keep for 2 weeks in the
refrigerator). Cook for 3–4 minutes, add the coconut milk,
gently simmer for 5 minutes.
Barbecue the lamb skewers for 5–10 minutes according to
how you like your meat cooked. Coat with massaman sauce.

Drink with: well-chilled Asian beer – yes, it's strong!

BASIL LAMB

With the friends you met on vacation

Serves 6
Preparation time 15 minutes
Cooking time 10 minutes over high heat

1 lb 12 oz lamb leg meat
Provençal salt (see page 18)
Basil oil:
1 bunch basil
1 lemon
1 teaspoon liquid honey
¾ cup olive oil
1 French shallot

Cut the lamb into 1¼ inch cubes. Thread these onto skewers
and rub them with the Provençal salt.
For the basil oil, pick the leaves off the basil, zest and juice the
lemon, process with the olive oil and honey. Peel the French
shallot, chop it up as finely as possible, add to the basil oil.
Barbecue the lamb skewers for 5–10 minutes according to
how you like the meat cooked. Coat them with basil oil.
Serve the Provençal salt on the side.

Drink with: the little rosé you bought together

LAMB, CUMIN AND ALMONDS

With someone who thinks that cumin goes with nothing

Serves 6
Preparation time 15 minutes
Marinating time 3 hours
Cooking time 10 minutes over high heat

1 lb 12 oz lamb leg meat
1½ cups flaked almonds
2 tablespoons cumin seeds
Marinade:
2 tablespoons maple syrup
¾ cup riesling
1 teaspoon coarsely ground black pepper
salt

Cut the lamb into 3 cm (1¼ inch) cubes. Toast the almonds
in a non-stick frying pan until they're golden brown.
For the marinade, combine the maple syrup with the
wine, add the cubes of lamb, season and allow to marinate
for 3 hours.
Thread the lamb onto skewers and roll them in the cumin.
Cook over high heat 5–10 minutes depending on how you
like the meat cooked. Scatter with flaked almonds.

Drink with: the rest of the riesling

VEAL AND GINGER SKEWERS

With your friends from up the coast

Serves 6
Preparation time 20 minutes
Cooking time 10 minutes over gentle heat

1 lb 12 oz veal schnitzels
18 medium mushrooms
3½ oz fresh ginger
⅔ cup vodka
Salt and pepper

Cut the veal schnitzels into small square slices of the same size. Cut the mushrooms into thick slices the same size as the pieces of veal. Peel the ginger, slice it thinly. Assemble the skewers, alternating meat, mushrooms and ginger. Cook for 10 minutes over gentle heat, season. Warm the vodka in a saucepan, flambé, pour the vodka over the skewers.

Drink with: the rest of the vodka over ice, it warms you up!

SNAIL-STYLE SKEWERS

With people who know how to take their time

Serves 6
Preparation time 20 minutes
Cooking time 8–9 minutes over high heat

1 lb 12 oz veal schnitzels
2 French shallots
1 bunch dill
1 teaspoon coarsely ground black pepper
Salt
Marinade:
3 tablespoons Savora mustard (or American mustard)
1 tablespoon olive oil
1 tablespoon vodka

Slice the veal schnitzels into ¾ inch thick strips. Peel and finely chop the French shallots, chop the dill. Combine the dill, French shallots and pepper, sprinkle this mixture over the strips of veal, season with salt. Roll up the strips like snails. Thread these snails on skewers.
For the marinade, combine the Savora mustard with the olive oil and vodka, spread this mixture over the skewers. Cook for 3–4 minutes over high heat, turn the skewers over.
Cook for a further 5 minutes.

Note: the barbecue grill needs to be very clean and hot so the mustard doesn't stick.

Drink with: an aromatic white with aromas of apple, acacia and apricot (or the rest of the vodka)

THE CLASSIC: HEART, LIVER, KIDNEY

With your adventurous friend

Serves 6
Preparation time 20 minutes
Cooking time 15 minutes over high heat

1 green pepper
1 red pepper
2 veal kidneys
7 oz beef heart
7 oz calf's liver
salt and pepper
Marinade:
½ cup tawny port
½ cup olive oil
1 teaspoon brown sugar

Cut the peppers into 1¼ inch squares. Peel and trim the fat from the kidneys, cut them into pieces the same size as the pieces of pepper. Cut up the heart in the same way. Peel the calf's liver and cut up in the same way.
For the marinade, combine the port with the olive oil and brown sugar. Add the meats, mix well.
Assemble the skewers, alternating the meats and differently colored pepper. Cook over high heat for about 15 minutes, turning the skewers regularly, season.

Drink with: creamy chablis with citrus on the nose

58
SKEWERS

CHICKEN HEART SKEWERS

With your lover—but watch out, that might change after the skewer

Serves 6
Preparation time 10 minutes
Cooking time 10 minutes over high heat

1 lb 5 oz chicken hearts
6 sprigs rosemary
Marinade:
1 teaspoon ground piment d'Espelette (or hot paprika)
1 teaspoon ground turmeric
1 teaspoon coarsely ground black pepper
⅔ cup olive oil
3 tablespoons rum
2 tablespoons sweet soy sauce

Trim fat from the chicken hearts.
For the marinade, combine the spices with the olive oil, rum, soy sauce. Add the chicken hearts, mix well.
Thread the chicken hearts onto the branches of rosemary and cook them over high heat for 10 minutes. Eat immediately.

Drink with: beaujolais (any kind)

KIDNEYS ON LICORICE

With your best friends

Serves 6
Preparation time 1 hour
Cooking time 10 minutes over high heat

3 pale veal kidneys
24 mushrooms
4 sticks of licorice root
Licorice sauce:
2 sticks of licorice root
2 cups cream
1 tablespoon sichuan peppercorns
3 tablespoons cognac
⅔ cup veal stock

Trim the fat from the kidneys, cut them into pieces. Halve the mushrooms. Split the 4 sticks of licorice root into sharp skewers. Assemble on the licorice root skewers, alternating mushrooms and pieces of kidney.
To make the licorice sauce, infuse the 2 sticks of licorice root in the cream, barely simmering, for 30 minutes. Set aside.

Toast the sichuan peppercorns in a dry saucepan, deglaze with cognac, flambé and add the veal stock as well as the licorice-infused cream. Reduce until you obtain a syrupy consistency. Cook the skewers for 10 minutes over high heat, coat them with licorice sauce.

Drink with: your best Bordeaux wine (or Premier grand cru) for the memories

VEAL SWEETBREAD SKEWERS

With special friends

Serves 6
Preparation time 1 hour
Cooking time 10 minutes over gentle heat

1 lb 5 oz veal sweetbreads (whole)
2 cups milk
12 fresh cep mushrooms ('champagne cork' or bouchon)
18 sundried tomatoes in oil
3 slices speck (smoked bacon or ham)
olive oil
salt and pepper

Blanch the sweetbreads in milk, bringing them to a bare simmer for 30 minutes. Peel the sweetbreads, removing any veins that should come away easily. Cut the sweetbreads into 1½ inch cubes. Wipe the cep mushrooms with a damp cloth and cut them in two.
Assemble the skewers, alternating the sundried tomatoes, ceps and sweetbreads. Season. Cook the speck on the barbecue until crispy and crumble it into pieces. Cook the skewers over gentle heat for 10 minutes. Drizzle over some olive oil and scatter with the crumbled speck.

Drink with: aged white burgundy with a clear botrytis influence

PEPPERED CALF'S LIVER

With a connoisseur

Serves 6
Preparation time 15 minutes
Marinating time 1 hour
Cooking time 5–6 minutes over high heat

1 lb 12 oz calf's liver
salt and pepper
Marinade:
⅔ cup olive oil
1 tablespoon very finely chopped rosemary leaves
3 tablespoons white balsamic vinegar
2 tablespoons Baies Rose or pink peppercorns (see Note)

Peel the calf's liver, removing the thin menbrane. Cut into
even 1¼ inch cubes.
For the marinade, combine the olive oil with the rosemary,
balsamic vinegar and pepper berries or peppercorns, add
the liver to this mixture and chill for 1 hour.
Thread the liver onto skewers and season. Cook over high
heat for 5–6 minutes, turning the skewers regularly.

Note: Baies Rose is a small pink berry from Brazil with
a sweet peppery taste.

Drink with: crisp white burgundy with an elegant finish

FISH SKEWERS

It's only one step from land to sea. It's summer, you're h
the waves play in unison, you've just pinched a monkfis
from them, pickpocketed a salmon…
The skewer is in the drink, fishing for compliments, sh
gets pickled, sings the blues, the iodine gets the upper
hand. It's reely good!

ROSEMARY-SKEWERED MONKFISH

With your friend Lolotte

Serves 6
Preparation time 15 minutes
Cooking time 6 minutes over high heat

2 lb 11 oz monkfish (or any firm fleshed fish)
6 branches of rosemary
salt and pepper
To drizzle:
3 lemons
½ cup olive oil
2 tablespoons glucose

Peel the monkfish and remove the central backbone. Remove any pin bones. Cut the monkfish into pieces of the same size. Whittle the branches of rosemary to a point, skewer the pieces of monkfish, rub with olive oil.
For the drizzle, zest the lemons, remove the skin and pith with a knife and extract the segments. Combine the zest, the lemon segments and the olive oil with the sugar syrup.
Sear the skewers for 3 minutes on each side. Drizzle with the lemon-sugar olive oil, season.

Drink with: sauvignon blanc with a light nose and a hint of herbs (of course!)

MONKFISH AND CHORIZO

With a foodie

Serves 6
Preparation time 15 minutes
Marinating time 3 hours
Cooking time 6 minutes over high heat

2 lb 11 oz monkfish (or any firm fleshed fish)
3½ oz spicy chorizo sausage
6 bulb spring onions
salt and pepper
Marinade:
1 vanilla bean, split with seeds scraped
1 cup coconut milk
Lemon olive oil:
½ cup olive oil
juice of one lemon

Peel the monkfish and remove the central backbone. Remove any pin bones. Cut the monkfish into pieces of the same size. For the marinade, add the scraped out vanilla bean and seeds to the coconut milk. Marinate the fish in the coconut milk mixture for 3 hours.
Cut the chorizo into thin slices and cut the bulb spring onions in two. On metal skewers, thread half a bulb spring onion, 1 piece of monkfish, 1 slice of chorizo, then monkfish, chorizo, monkfish, chorizo…Finish with another half a bulb spring onion.
Sear the skewers for 3 minutes on each side. Drizzle with olive oil mixed with lemon juice, season.

Drink with: an obscure white with the essence of spring

SESAME SALMON

With someone whose heart you want to open up!

Serves 6
Preparation time 15 minutes
Cooking time 2 minutes over high heat

2 lb 4 oz fresh salmon
5 tablespoons sesame oil
1 tablespoon pastis (aniseed flavored liqueur)
1¾ oz fresh ginger
1 bunch basil
3 tablespoons sesame seeds

Remove the bones from the salmon and cut it into bite-sized pieces. Combine the sesame oil with the pastis. Brush the salmon pieces with this mixture. Peel the ginger and cut into thin slices. Pick the leaves from the basil. Thread onto small skewers 1 slice of ginger, 1 piece of salmon, 1 basil leaf, then ginger, salmon, basil, salmon, ginger. Roll the skewers in the sesame seeds. Sear 1 minute on each side.

Drink with: a smooth and fruity white with stony citrus nose

LEMON SALMON

With your town friends back in the country

Serves 6
Preparation time 10 minutes
Cooking time 2 minutes over high heat

1 lb 12 oz fresh salmon
3 lemons
Marinade:
2 tablespoons honey
4 tablespoons light soy sauce
4 tablespoons lemon juice
1 pinch ground piment d'Espelette (or hot paprika)

Remove the bones from the salmon, cut it into bite-sized cubes. Cut each lemon into 12 segments.
For the marinade, combine all of the marinade ingredients. Reserve some for sauce.
Roll the pieces of salmon in the remaining marinade. Thread 1 lemon segment and 1 piece of salmon onto wooden toothpicks. You should obtain 36 small skewers. Sear 1 minute each side. Coat with reserved marinade.

Drink with: complex white burgundy with intense buttery and melon flavors

OLIVE-BASIL SALMON

With another forty-something (like salmon returning to the source)

Serves 6
Preparation time 20 minutes
Cooking time 5 minutes over high heat

zest of 1 lemon
¾ cup olive oil
1 salmon fillet
30 pitted black dry-salted olives
12 anchovy fillets in oil, chopped
1 bunch basil, leaves stripped (30 leaves)

Chop the lemon zest and combine it with the olive oil.
Set aside.
Using a long knife, remove the skin from the salmon, remove any bones and cut it into 4 x ¾ inch strips. Stuff each olive with a piece of anchovy. Roll each olive in a basil leaf, wrap it in a strip of salmon. Skewer with a toothpick or small bamboo skewer to hold it in place. Sear the skewers for 5 minutes on each side. Serve drizzled with the lemon oil.

Drink with: grenache-based blend that is rich and bold

YAKITORI

Yakitori are small Japanese skewers grilled over high heat. Yakitori means 'grilled bird.'

They are not however made up of sparrows, robins or other songbirds, but rather of meat, fish, seafood and vegetables. These little skewers are the ideal complement to a cocktail that goes into overtime.

They are dipped in different sauces, the most well-known being teriyaki sauce, which is used for meat and fish as well as chicken. They are enjoyed in bite-sized servings on small wooden skewers, kushis.

You should allow at least six yakitori per person for a full meal, mixing meats and fish to satisfy everyone's appetite. Yakitori are cooked quickly over high heat so that the food is well seared and the sauce caramelizes. Bon appétit!

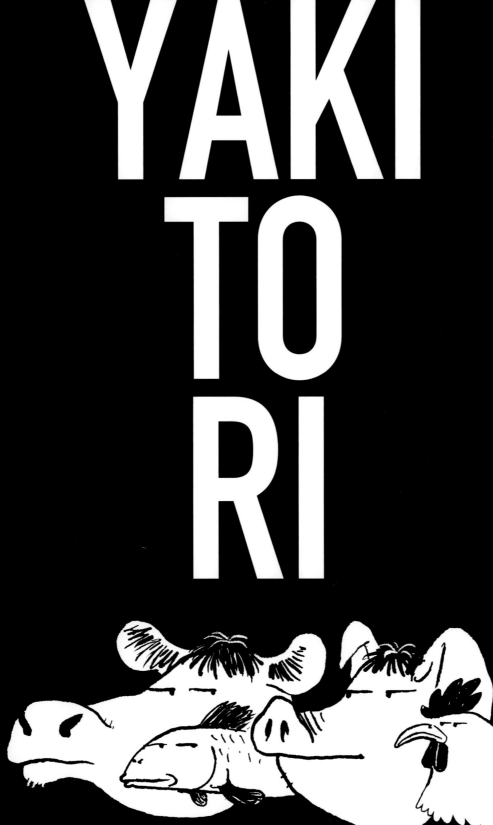

FISH YAKITORI

For 6 yakitori
Preparation time 5 minutes
Cooking time 5 minutes

SHRIMP

6 jumbo shrimp
1 teaspoon fennel seeds
½ cup olive oil
½ cup soy sauce
1 tablespoon brown sugar

Peel the shrimp. Crush the fennel seeds in a mortar and pestle. Combine all of the ingredients. Dip the shrimp into this mixture, thread them onto skewers, cook 5 minutes.

HAKE

14 oz hake (or cod)
⅔ cup soy sauce
1 teaspoon ground cumin
1 teaspoon balsamic vinegar
1 tablespoon molasses

Cut the hake into thick strips and thread these onto skewers. Combine all remaining ingredients and coat the fish with this marinade. Cook for 5 minutes.

SALMON

10½ oz fresh salmon
½ bunch cilantro
1 French shallot
1 lemongrass stem
1 tablespoon tamarind sauce
salt and pepper

Remove the bones and skin of the salmon. Pick the leaves from the cilantro. Peel the French shallot, chop it up finely, chop the lemongrass. Process everything together and add the tamarind, season. Shape small sausages of the mixture around the skewers, cook for 5 minutes.

SCALLOPS

6 scallops
2 tablespoons sweet soy sauce
1 tablespoon poppy seeds
juice of 1 lime

Remove the roe from the scallops (if necessary), coat them with the sweet soy sauce. Thread the scallops onto the skewers, cook for 2–3 minutes. Serve with the poppyseeds, drizzle with lime juice.

MEAT YAKITORI

For 6 yakitori

DUCK BREAST

1 duck breast
1 garlic clove
2 tablespoons ketchup
2 tablespoons soy sauce
1 tablespoon molasses

Remove the fat from the duck breast and slice into thin strips. Peel the garlic, chop it finely. Combine all of the ingredients including the duck strips. Thread the duck strips onto the skewers, cook for 3 minutes.

BEEF COMTÉ

7 oz rump steak
2 tablespoons soy sauce
2 tablespoons Savora mustard (or American mustard)
5½ oz comté cheese (or Gruyère)
2 tablespoons sesame seeds

Cut the meat into thin strips, 2 inch wide.
Combine the soy sauce and the Savora mustard, dip the meat into this mixture. Cut the comté cheese into strips, thread them lengthways onto the skewers then wind the beef around the cheese. Sprinkle with sesame seeds. Cook for 3–4 minutes or until the comté begins to melt.

CHICKEN

2 chicken breast fillets
2 French shallots
½ bunch cilantro
2 tablespoons créme fraiche or Greek yogurt
1 tablespoon olive oil
salt and pepper

Cut the chicken lengthways and thread onto skewers. Peel the French shallots, chop them finely, chop the cilantro.
Combine all the flavoring ingredients with the créme fraiche, add the olive oil, season. Roll the yakitori in this mixture, cook for 5 minutes.

VEAL

2 thick veal escalopes
1 tablespoon brown sugar
juice of one lemon
⅔ cup sweet soy sauce
1 tablespoon ketchup
salt and pepper

Cut the escalopes into thick strips and thread them onto skewers. Combine the remaining ingredients. Dip the yakitori in the sauce, cook for 5 minutes. Season.

CHAPTER II

SAUSAGES

The famous sausage is one of the essentials of the barbecue. It keeps us company from the first glimmers of the embers to the last glimmers of those same embers. Gather round unexpected friends, buddies from the office, the baseball team that's invited itself over, and the sausage party is up and running. Be careful.

Beneath its friendly appearance, the sausage demands a special vigilance when it comes to cooking. The coals must be both hot enough to sear the sausages and gentle enough to cook them through. Drops of fat in contact with the embers tend to turn the barbecue into a gigantic bonfire. It is therefore preferable to cook sausages on a grill slightly away from the coals. We all have memories of a pre-game hotdog one afternoon during the football championship that was burned on the outside and raw on the inside!

THE PANORAMA OF SAUSAGES

When you're talking sausages, you're talking vast choice.
There are as many varieties as there are butchers.
In France we have:
- the Strasbourg sausage: smooth texture, red color.
- the knack: smooth texture, orangey color.
- the Frankfurt sausage: smooth texture, smoky flavor, orangey color.
- the Morteau sausage: large smoked sausage, coarse texture, poach before grilling.
- the Montbéliard sausage: smoked, cumin flavour, coarse texture, poach before grilling.
- the Toulouse sausage: large sausage, coarse texture.
- the Lyon cervelas sausage: large sausage, coarse texture, flavored with truffles and pistachios, poach before grilling.
- the sabodet sausage: large pig's-head sausage, poach before grilling.
- the chipolata sausage: thin sausage often flavored with herbs, coarse texture.
- the diot sausage: garlic-flavored sausage from the Savoy, coarse texture.
- the merguez sausage: spicy sausage using beef and mutton, no pork.
Many of these can be found in delicatessens and good food stores.

HOME-MADE SAUSAGES

You don't need to be a butcher to make the sausage of your choice at home. Forget the equipment (grinder, filler attachments…), use your hands and the deed is done.

Base recipe for 6 sausages
Preparation time 20 minutes
Resting time 24 hours

EXOTIC

1 French shallot
1¾ oz fresh ginger
1 bunch cilantro
½ bunch tarragon
1 lb 2 oz ground pork
salt and pepper
caul fat, very well rinsed

Peel the French shallot and the ginger, pick the leaves from the herbs. Chop everything finely, combine it with the meat and season. Shape into sausages with your hands and roll them in the caul fat. Refrigerate for 24 hours before cooking.

GOAT'S CHEESE

1 picodon cheese (goat's milk cheese)
6 sage leaves
1 tablespoon blanched almonds
1 lb 2 oz ground pork
1 tablespoon herbes de Provence (usually marjoram, oregano, rosemary, thyme)
salt and pepper
caul fat, very well rinsed

Finely chop the picodon cheese, sage leaves and almonds. Combine these with the meat, add the herbes de Provence, season. Shape into sausages with your hands and roll them in the caul fat. Refrigerate for 24 hours before cooking.

BACK FROM THE WOODS

5½ oz cep mushrooms ('champagne cork' or bouchon)
3 garlic cloves
2 tablespoons olive oil
1 lb 2 oz ground pork
salt and pepper
caul fat, very well rinsed

Wipe the cep mushrooms to remove any soil (don't wash them). Cut them into ½ inch cubes. Peel and chop the garlic. Sauté the mushrooms in the olive oil for 5 minutes with the garlic. Combine this mixture with the meat and season. Shape into sausages with your hands and roll them in the caul fat. Refrigerate for 24 hours before cooking.

MEDITERRANEAN

2 large onions
1 oz black pitted Kalamata olives
1¾ oz sundried tomatoes
2 tablespoons olive oil
3 garlic cloves, peeled and chopped finely
1 sprig of fresh thyme, leaves chopped very finely
salt and pepper
1 lb 2 oz ground pork
caul fat, very well rinsed

Peel the onions and finely chop them. Roughly chop the olives and the sundried tomatoes. In a frying pan, soften the onions in the olive oil, add the olives, garlic, thyme leaves and stew together. Combine this mixture with the meat and season. Shape into sausages with your hands and roll them in the caul fat. Refrigerate for 24 hours before cooking.

CAILLETTES

**With two foodies ready to take on your choice
of ingredient argument**

Serves 6
Preparation time 45 minutes
Cooking time 20 minutes over gentle heat

1 bunch Swiss chard
4 bulb spring onions
½ cup olive oil
salt and pepper
1 lb 12 oz ground pork
caul fat, very well rinsed

Chop the stem and leaves of the Swiss chard as finely as
possible. Chop the bulb spring onions, including the green
part.
Gently sauté the Swiss chard and spring onions in the olive oil
for 15 minutes. The Swiss chard stem should be tender. Cool.
Combine the Swiss chard-onion preparation with the meat,
season well. Roll into balls the size of a tennis ball and wrap
them in caul fat. You can make one large caillette per person
or two smaller ones. Refrigerate for 24 hours before cooking.
Cook over gentle heat for 20 minutes, turning them regularly.

**Drink with: sexy red full of plums, boysenberry and white
pepper aromas**

SAUSAGE IN THE EMBERS

With a full-blood sausage connoisseur to pay him homage

Serves 6
Preparation time 15 minutes
Cooking time 30 minutes over gentle heat

2 fresh Lyon sausages (or other blood sausages)
2 large slices of speck (smoked ham or bacon)
2 bay leaves
4 cloves
6 garlic cloves, unpeeled
6 French shallots
1 teaspoon quatre-épices (see Note)
1⅔ cup beaujolais
2¾ oz butter

Make two large parcels out of foil, the same length as the
sausages. In each of the parcels arrange 1 sausage, 1 slice
of speck, 1 bay leaf, 2 cloves, 3 garlic cloves and 3 French
shallots. Combine the spices with the beaujolais, divide the
wine between the parcels and add half the butter to each.
Seal each parcel airtight and place the parcels over gentle
heat for 30 minutes. Slice the sausage, accompany each
serving with one of the cooked shallots and one of the garlic
cloves and coat with the wine sauce from the foil parcels.

Note: quatre-épices literally means four spices and is common
in France. It's a mixture of two parts ground white pepper, one
part each of ground ginger, ground nutmeg and ground cloves.

**Drink with: vibrant ruby red beaujolais (what's left of
the above)**

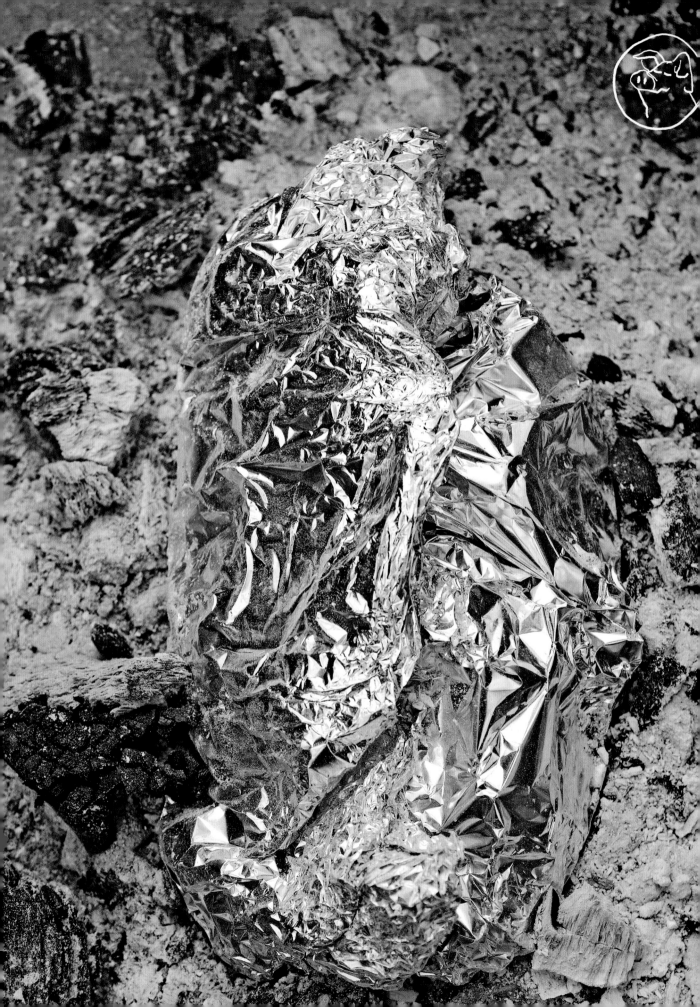

CUSTOMIZED MERGUEZ

With your friend from the game in memory of that last hotdog you ate at the stadium

Serves 6
Preparation time 20 minutes
Cooking time 10 minutes over gentle heat

18 merguez sausages
1 teaspoon ground cinnamon
1 apple
1 orange
caul fat, very well rinsed

Remove the skin from the merguez, work the meat with a fork to loosen the texture, add the cinnamon. Peel the apple and cut into small cubes. Juice and zest the orange, combine with the apples then the merguez meat. Shape mixture into ovals 3¼ inches long, roll them in the caul fat. Refrigerate for 24 hours before cooking.
Cook them over gentle heat for 10 minutes.

Drink with: a good icy-cold beer to commemorate…

CHAPTER III

FILLETS
&
ROASTS

CHICKEN BREAST WITH COCONUT MILK

With your girlfriend

Serves 6
Preparation time 20 minutes
Resting time 3 hours
Cooking time 5 minutes over high heat

6 free-range chicken breast fillets
2 limes
salt and pepper
Coconut milk marinade:
1¾ oz fresh ginger
2 French shallots
2 garlic cloves
2 tablespoons sunflower oil
1 tablespoon sugar
1½ cups coconut milk
1 bunch chives

Slice the chicken breasts into thin strips. Juice and zest
the limes, sprinkle the juice and zest over the chicken.
For the marinade, peel the ginger, French shallots and garlic.
Chop them all up then gently sauté in the oil for 5 minutes,
adding the sugar. Off the heat, pour in the coconut milk.
Snip the chives into ½ inch lengths and add them
to the mixture. Pour this mixture over the chicken and chill
for 3 hours.
Cook the chicken over high heat until well browned.
Serve coated with the rest of the marinade.

**Drink with: gorgeous rosé with the color of summer
sunset (slightly chilled)**

DUCK TENDERLOINS À L'ORANGE

With friends you want to amaze

Serves 6
Preparation time 15 minutes
Marinating time 3 hours
Cooking time 5 minutes over high heat

1 lb 12 oz duck tenderloins or skinned duck
  breasts, cut into strips
salt and pepper
Marinade:
2 oranges
⅔ cup wine vinegar
2 tablespoons sugar
2 tablespoons Grand Marnier
Orange salad with red onions:
2 oranges
2 red onions
3 scallions
3 tablespoons olive oil

For the marinade, juice and zest the 2 oranges. Heat the vinegar with the sugar until it caramelizes, add the orange juice and zests, then the Grand Marnier. Cool. Place the duck tenderloins in this mixture and chill for 3 hours.
For the salad, remove the skin and pith of the 2 oranges to obtain the segments. Peel and finely chop the red onions, slice the scallions thinly. Combine all the salad ingredients with the olive oil.
Cook the tenderloins for 5 minutes over high heat.
Combine with the orange and red onion salad, season.

Drink with: deep dark purple cabernet with a soft finish

DUCK TENDERLOINS WITH SUMMER VEGETABLES

With people in a hurry

Serves 6
Preparation time 10 minutes
Cooking time 10 minutes on the barbecue hot plate

3 garlic cloves
4 large onions

12 long mild chilies, red and green
3 young zucchinis
1 lb 5 oz duck tenderloins or skinned duck
  breasts cut into strips
1 small jar or can baby corn (unsweetened)
2 tablespoons balsamic vinegar
3 tablespoons soy sauce
olive oil

Peel and finely slice the garlic and onions. Halve the chilies, remove the seeds. Cut the zucchini into even lengths. Sauté the onions and garlic on the barbecue hot plate in a little olive oil, add the duck tenderloins and barbecue 3–4 minutes. Then add the rest of the vegetables and cook for 5 minutes more, stirring well. Deglaze with the balsamic vinegar and soy sauce. Serve immediately.

Drink with: pale and delicate rosé

SWEET-SOUR CHICKEN DRUMSTICKS

With your ex at the end of a bittersweet affair

Serves 6
Preparation time 15 minutes
Cooking time 20 minutes over gentle heat

12 chicken drumsticks
salt
Sweet-sour sauce:
5 garlic cloves
1 red onion
3½ oz fresh pineapple
½ cup sugar
2 tablespoons rice vinegar
4 tablespoons ketchup

For the sauce, peel the garlic and onion, slice them thinly. Process all of the sauce ingredients together to make a smooth purée. Cook this preparation over a low heat in a frying pan for 5 minutes. It should start to caramelize. Season. Set some of the sauce aside to use for dipping.
Dip the drumsticks in the remainder of the sauce, cook them over gentle heat for 20 minutes, turning them regularly. Serve with the reserved sweet-sour sauce.

Drink with: champagne (the real stuff!)

FILLETS & ROASTS

EPIGRAMS OF LAMB WITH TAMARIND

With someone who's not afraid to get their hands dirty

Serves 6
Preparation time 15 minutes
Resting time 3 hours
Cooking time 20 minutes over gentle heat

6 lamb epigrams (boned breast pieces)
Marinade:
4 bulb spring onions
1 tablespoon tamarind paste
3 tablespoons ketchup
2 tablespoons sunflower oil
6 tablespoons soy sauce
1 teaspoon ground cumin
1 tablespoon brown sugar
juice of 2 lemons
salt and pepper

For the marinade, finely chop the bulb spring onions. Combine all of the marinade ingredients together to make a smooth mixture. Cover the lamb epigrams with this mixture and chill, covered for 3 hours.
Cook over gentle heat for 20 minutes, turning the epigrams regularly and coating them regularly with marinade.

Drink with: simple rosé blend (with a hint of merlot, perhaps)

RABBIT THIGHS WITH SUNDRIED TOMATOES

With someone who doesn't ask questions

Serves 6
Preparation time 20 minutes
Marinating time 24 hours
Cooking time 30 minutes over gentle heat

6 lovely rabbit thighs
assorted heirloom tomatoes
⅓ cup olive oil
½ tablespoon herbes de Provence (usually marjoram, oregano, rosemary, thyme)
salt and pepper

Marinade:
5½ oz sundried tomatoes in oil
2 garlic cloves
½ tablespoon herbes de Provence (usually marjoram, oregano, rosemary, thyme)
¼ oz fresh ginger
⅓ cup olive oil

The day before, prepare the marinade. Process together the sundried tomatoes, peeled garlic, herbes de Provence, ginger and olive oil until you have a paste. Season. Make a series of regular incisions in the rabbit thighs down to the bone. Fill with the tomato paste, wrap the thighs tightly in plastic wrap and chill for 24 hours.
Cook the rabbit over gentle heat for 15 minutes on each side, turning regularly. Brush the tomatoes with the olive oil, add the herbes de Provence, season. Barbecue the tomatoes for 5 minutes.

Drink with: cabernet with blackberry aroma

BEEF SHOULDER MARINATED IN CANOLA OIL

With a vampire

Serves 6
Preparation time 15 minutes
Marinating 24 hours
Cooking time 3 minutes over high heat

2 lb 4 oz beef shoulder
Marinade:
12 bulb spring onions
1 bunch basil, leaves reserved
2 tablespoons maple syrup
1¼ cups canola oil
1 teaspoon tandoori spices
1 teaspoon fennel seeds
juice of one lemon
salt and pepper

Cut the beef into thin slices across the grain of the meat.
For the marinade, finely slice the bulb spring onions as well as the basil leaves. Combine all of the marinade ingredients, reserve a little for serving. Cover the beef with the remaining mixture and cover with plastic film. Chill for 24 hours.
Quickly sear the beef shoulder over high heat.
Serve immediately with the reserved marinade.

Drink with: something blood red

BONED SADDLE
OF RABBIT

With your large rabbit because you like him very much

Serves 6
Preparation time 20 minutes
Cooking time 20 minutes over gentle heat

3 saddles of rabbit
caul fat, very well rinsed
salt and pepper
Stuffing:
1 French shallot
1 bunch basil
1¾ oz sundried tomatoes in oil
3 artichokes in oil
1 scallion
1 slice of stale sandwich bread

Bone the saddles of rabbit, taking care not to damage the meat.
Lay the saddles out flat, season.
For the stuffing, peel the French shallot, slice it thickly, pick
the leaves from the basil. Process all of the stuffing ingredients
together to make a paste.
Place the stuffing between the loin and the flap of the saddle,
close over the flap, roll in the caul fat. Cook over gentle heat
for 20 minutes turning the rabbit regularly.

Drink with: rich and weighty cabernet sauvignon

PORK FILLETS WITH PISTACHIO PESTO

With your Italian butcher

Serves 6
Preparation time 30 minutes
Cooking time 20 minutes over gentle heat

3 pork fillets
salt and pepper
Pistachio pesto:
1 bunch basil
3 garlic cloves
3½ oz good parmesan cheese
1 slice of stale country bread
3½ oz shelled pistachios
¾ cup olive oil

Carefully butterfly the fillets by slicing them lengthways.
For the pesto, pick the leaves from the basil. Peel the garlic,
cut the parmesan into cubes. Crumble the bread. Process all
of the pesto ingredients together to obtain a fairly coarse paste.
Season the fillets, fill them with pistachio pesto, roll them back
up to enclose the filling. Tie them up with cooking twine
soaked in salted water. Cook over gentle heat for 20 minutes,
turning them regularly.

Drink with: Italian chianti

LIKE A PAUPIETTE WITH SWEET ONIONS

With the village brass band

Serves 6
Preparation time 40 minutes
Cooking time 10 minutes over gentle heat

6 thin veal schnitzels
Onion confit:
4 mild sweet onions
2 garlic cloves
1¾ oz black olives
1 bunch cilantro
1 tablespoon pine nuts
1 tablespoon ground cumin
½ cup olive oil
salt and pepper

For the confit, peel the onions and garlic and slice them.
Roughly chop the black olives, pick the leaves from the cilantro
and chop them. Gently sauté the onions and garlic in the olive
oil with the black olives, pine nuts, cumin and cilantro for 10
minutes. The onions should stew down. Season.
Lay out the veal schnitzels and season them. Divide the onion
confit between the six schnitzels, close them up around the
filling like 'paupiettes' and tie them with cooking twine soaked
in salted water. Cook over gentle heat for 10 minutes.

Drink with: viognier with good intensity on the nose

DUCK BREAST & ZUCCHINI TOURNEDOS

With the little one's football team

Serves 6
Preparation time 30 minutes
Cooking time 10 minutes over gentle heat

3 duck breasts
3 young zucchini
salt
Cep mushroom powder:
1¾ oz dried cep mushrooms ('champagne
  cork' or bouchon) or porcini
2 tablespoons coarsely ground black pepper
1 tablespoon herbes de Provence (usually
  marjoram, oregano, rosemary, thyme)

For the mushroom powder, process the dried cep mushrooms until finely ground, combine them with the pepper and herbes de Provence.
Cut the duck breasts lengthways into ⅛ inch wide strips.
Lay out the strips of duck two by two on top of each other, alternating layers of fat and lean. Cut the zucchini into strips using a vegetable peeler. Lay the strips of zucchini on top of the duck, season with the mushroom powder and season with salt. Roll up the strips tightly to make tournedos and tie with string. Make 6 tournedos in this way. Cook over gentle heat 5 minutes each side.

Drink with: cabernet sauvignon and merlot blend (magnum bottle)

VEAL ROULADE WITH JAMÓN

With a flamenco dancer

Serves 6
Preparation time 20 minutes
Cooking time 10 minutes over gentle heat

6 thin veal schnitzels
6 slices of jamón Serrano (dry-cured
  Spanish ham)
pepper
Anchovy stuffing:
1 French shallot
12 anchovies in oil
1 bunch tarragon
1¾ oz parmesan cheese
½ cup olive oil
½ cup shelled walnuts

For the stuffing, peel the French shallot, chop it finely.
Roughly chop the anchovies. Process together the tarragon,
parmesan, olive oil and walnuts. Add the pieces of anchovy
and the chopped shallot.
Lay the schnitzels out flat, season them with pepper. Place
a slice of jamón on each schnitzel, then the anchovy mixture.
Roll up the schnitzels and tie them with cooking twine soaked
in salted water. Cook over gentle heat for 10 minutes, turning
the schnitzels regularly.

Drink with: best chardonnay on the shelf

BUTTERFLIED LAMB SHOULDER

With the guests at your anniversary

Serves 6
Preparation time 20 minutes
Cooking time 45 minutes over gentle heat

2 lamb shoulders
salt with Moroccan spices
12 sage leaves
¾ cup olive oil
2 lb 4 oz eggplants

Bone the lamb shoulders, butterfly them out flat and rub with the spiced salt. Finely slice the sage leaves, combine them with the olive oil, set aside at room temperature. Cut the eggplants into rounds.
Barbecue the lamb shoulders over gentle heat for 45 minutes.
Barbecue the rounds of eggplant for 3–4 minutes.
Serve everything with the sage oil.

Drink with: at least five-year-old red, it's your anniversary after all

PEPPERMINT LAMB LEG STEAK

With a Brit in exile

Serves 6
Preparation time 15 minutes
Cooking time 10 minutes over high heat and on the hotplate

6 lamb leg steaks
Vegetables:
6 garlic cloves
1¾ oz fresh ginger
6 French shallots
2 tablespoons olive oil
1 bunch peppermint, leaves torn
salt and pepper

To prepare the vegetables, peel and roughly slice the garlic, ginger and French shallots. Gently sauté the French shallots with the garlic and ginger in the olive oil for 7–8 minutes, add the torn peppermint leaves just before serving, season. Barbecue the lamb steaks over high heat. The cooking time will depend how you like the lamb cooked. Serve with the vegetables.

Drink with: elegant merlot blend with a lingering finish

GARLIC-STUDDED LAMB LEG STEAK

With whoever you like, but not for a tête-à-tête

Serves 6
Preparation time 15 minutes
Cooking time 10 minutes over high heat

12 black Kalamata olives
6 garlic cloves
2 branches of rosemary
12 anchovies in oil
6 lamb leg steaks
pepper

Pit the black olives. Peel and quarter the garlic cloves and remove the sprout in the middle. Cut the rosemary into small tufts.
Cut the anchovies in two.
Make small incisions in the lamb steaks using a pointed knife. Insert garlic, olives, anchovies and rosemary. Cook over high heat for 5 minutes on each side. Season with pepper, place the salt on the table (the anchovies already give quite a salty taste).

Drink with: cabernet merlot with silky tannins

SADDLE OF LAMB

With a delicate cyclist

Serves 6
Preparation time 30 minutes
Cooking time 20 minutes over gentle heat

1 beautiful saddle of lamb
1 bunch basil
2 French shallots
salt and pepper
Garlic-hazelnut purée:
8 garlic cloves
¾ cup milk
1 tablespoon hazelnuts

Bone the saddle of lamb, separating the two loins.
For the purée, peel the garlic, cook it for 15 minutes
in the milk. Strain and discard the milk. Purée the garlic.
Roughly crush the hazelnuts. Combine the garlic purée
with the hazelnuts.
Pick the leaves from the basil, peel and finely chop the French
shallots. Lay out the two halves of the saddle, skin side down.
Spread the inside with the garlic-hazelnut purée, add the basil
and the finely chopped French shallots and season.
Close the flaps of the saddle over the loin and tie closed
with string. Cook over gentle heat for 20 minutes, turning
the saddle regularly.

**Drink with: an organic wine, it won't leave any traces in the
drug test**

SCHNITZEL AND AGED COMTÉ

With a boxer on the come-back

Serves 6
Preparation time 30 minutes
Cooking time 7–8 minutes over gentle heat

3 veal schnitzels, ½ inch thick
salt
7 oz aged Comté cheese (or Gruyére)
caul fat, very well rinsed
Marinade:
1 tablespoon honey
1 tablespoon white port
1 teaspoon sichuan peppercorns
1 tablespoon fennel seeds

For the marinade, combine the honey with the port, pepper and fennel seeds.
Chop the veal schnitzels into ½ inch cubes, put them in the marinade and season with salt.
Cut the Comté cheese into cubes the same size as the veal. Thread onto skewers, alternating meat and cheese. Roll each skewer tightly in the caul fat. Cook over gentle heat for 10 minutes, turning the skewers regularly.

Drink with: cool climate white

SPECK

With your old uncle and aunt, who love a bit of pork

Serves 6
Preparation time 10 minutes
Cooking time 10 minutes over gentle heat

2 bulb spring onions
1 baguette
2 garlic cloves
½ cup canola oil
6 beautiful fresh tomatoes
1 bunch basil
12 slices of speck (smoked ham or bacon),
  ¼ inch thick

Finely slice the bulb spring onions. Cut the baguette into slices lengthways. Peel the garlic and rub it over the slices of bread. Drizzle the baguette with some canola oil. Slice the tomatoes, roughly slice the basil. Barbecue the slices of speck for 5 minutes on each side and toast the slices of baguette. Serve everything tapas-style.

Drink with: well-chilled cask of rosé (they'll be sleeping over anyway)

VEAL FLANK AND SARASSOU

With a seasoned camper who needs new recipes

Serves 6
Preparation time 15 minutes
Cooking time 30 minutes over gentle heat

6 slices of veal flank (or boned breast)
spicy salt (see page 18)
Sarassou:
2 French shallots
1 bunch radishes
1 celery stalk
9 oz sarassou or créme fraiche
  or Greek yogurt
sea salt and coarsely ground black pepper

Remove the cartilage from the veal flank, rub the meat with the spicy salt. Barbecue the veal over gentle heat 15 minutes on each side: they should be nice and brown.
For the sarassou, peel the French shallots and chop them finely. Slice the radishes and celery. Combine all of these with the sarassou, season with sea salt and coarsely ground black pepper. Serve the sarassou over the cooked veal.

Drink with: slam dunk red

SANDWICH-STYLE DUCK BREAST

With Jacky, obviously

Serves 6
Preparation time 15 minutes
Cooking time 15 minutes over gentle heat

1 red onion
5½ oz sheep's milk cheese
3 duck breasts
salt and pepper
2 tablespoons ketchup

Peel and slice the red onion. Thinly slice the sheep's milk cheese. Using a sharp knife, slash the skin side of the duck breasts in a criss-cross pattern. Cut the breasts in two, season. Place some cheese, onion and ketchup on one half, cover with the other half and tie with cooking twine soaked in salted water. Cook over gentle heat, set back so that the fat doesn't catch alight, 6–7 minutes on each side.

Drink with: cabernet sauvignon and Jacky, obviously

ANDOUILLETTE
EN PAPILLOTE

With your local politician (andouillette is like politics, it should smell a bit like sh*t, but not too much)

Serves 6
Preparation time 15 minutes
Cooking time 15 minutes over gentle heat

6 French shallots
6 andouillettes (French sausages)
6 garlic cloves
1 bunch lemon thyme
1¼ cups chénas-style beaujolais
1¼ cups tawny port
4¼ oz butter
salt and pepper

Peel the French shallots. Make parcels out of foil. Place
1 andouillette in each parcel, add 1 unpeeled garlic clove,
1 French shallot and a little lemon thyme. Divide the
beaujolais, port and butter between the parcels, season.
Seal the parcels airtight, place them over gentle heat for
15 minutes. Serve the parcels on the plate.

Drink with: beaujoulais of breadth and substance (unlike the politician)

BURGERS

The hamburger is no doubt the most global sandwich ever created. Its origins date back to the nineteenth century with the departure of Germans from the port of Hamburg towards a welcoming America. This sandwich, made of cooked minced meat served between two pieces of bread, became the standard dish of these trans-Atlantic crossings. Once in the United States, 'steak cooked Hamburg-style' quickly found a place in the restaurants around New York harbor. It attracted a number of homesick Germans, but also people from all corners of the globe.

The hamburger is born, and starts its international rise. It will first spread throughout the United States, in particular in 1931, with the appearance in the Popeye comics of the character of Wimpy, a true hamburger lover, which gives rise to the idea of a chain of restaurants dedicated to the dish. This enjoys rapid success, competitors rush to follow, the concept of a low priced, quickly served meal in itself becoming its hallmark. Its return to Europe in the 1970s marks the conclusion of its epic tale, and it is forever lodged in posterity. The hamburger today is synonymous with globalization.

THE TRUE BURGER

The basic components of the hamburger are: ground meat, a soft and slightly sweet bun with sesame seeds, sweet onion, tomato ketchup, sweet-sour pickles, slices of cheddar cheese, bacon and lettuce.

CLASSIC

For 6 hamburgers
Preparation time 10 minutes
Cooking time 5 minutes over high heat

1 sweet onion
6 hamburger patties
6 slices bacon
6 hamburger buns
3 tablespoons ketchup
6 slices cheddar cheese
6 small lettuce leaves or a mixture
 of baby leaves

Slice the onion. Cook the hamburger patties, onion and the bacon over high heat. Toast the buns on the barbecue. Spread the buns with some ketchup and assemble the hamburgers, alternating all of the ingredients: cheddar, hamburger, bacon, onion, lettuce.

HAM

For 6 hamburgers
Preparation time 10 minutes
Cooking time 10 minutes over high heat

5½ oz Comté cheese (or Gruyére)
3 bulb spring onions
3 thick slices of ham
6 thin slices of belly pork
6 hamburger buns
3½ oz sundried tomatoes
1 bunch cilantro
Sauce:
3 tablespoons mayonnaise
3 tablespoons ketchup
1 tablespoon cognac

Using a vegetable peeler, make slivers of Comté cheese.
Slice the bulb spring onions. Cut the slices of ham in two.
Cook the ham and the belly pork on the barbecue for
5 minutes. Lay the slices of Comté on top of the ham, leave
to melt in peace.
For the sauce, combine the mayonnaise with the ketchup
and cognac.
Toast the buns on the barbecue, spread with sauce and
assemble the burger with layers of ham, Comté, onions, pork,
sundried tomatoes, cilantro.

CHICKEN

For 6 hamburgers
Preparation time 5 minutes
Cooking time 10 minutes over gentle heat on the hot plate

2 red onions
6 spears of green asparagus
6 hamburger buns
olive oil
6 chicken breast fillets
10½ oz roquefort cheese
arugula
salt and pepper

Peel and slice the onions, cut the aparagus spears in four and
cook the onions and asparagus on the hot plate until golden
brown. Drizzle the buns with some olive oil. Toast them on
the barbecue. Cook the chicken breasts for 7–8 minutes.
Cut the roquefort cheese into 6 slices, allow them to barely
melt on the hotplate. Dress the arugula with olive oil, salt and
pepper. Assemble the hamburger, making layers of asparagus,
chicken, roquefort, onions, arugula.

FOIE GRAS

For 6 hamburgers
Preparation time 10 minutes
Cooking time 10 minutes over gentle heat on the hotplate

2 duck breast fillets
1¾ oz baby spinach leaves
6 hamburger buns
6 slices fresh foie gras
3 tablespoons wholegrain mustard
salt and pepper

Slash the skin of the duck breasts in a criss-cross pattern down
to the flesh. Cook the duck breasts over gentle heat 5 minutes
skin side, 2 minutes flesh side (they should stay red). Cut them
into thin slices.
Arrange the baby spinach leaves on a plate, cover them with
the duck breast. Toast the buns on the barbecue, cook the
slices of foie gras on the hot plate for about 1 minute on each
side. Spread the buns with mustard, assemble the hamburger
by piling on the duck, foie gras and spinach. Season.

EGG

For 6 hamburgers
Preparation time 15 minutes
Cooking time 10 minutes over high heat on the hot plate

1 sweet onion
1 cucumber
2 tomatoes
6 hamburger patties (ground beef)
6 slices of speck (smoked ham or bacon)
6 hamburger buns
6 eggs
3 large spoonfuls Savora mustard
  (or American mustard)
3 tablespoons ketchup

Peel the onion, slice it with the cucumber and tomatoes.
Cook the hamburgers over high heat as well as the slices
of speck. Toast the buns on the barbecue grill, cook the eggs
on the hot plate. Spread the buns with mustard and ketchup.
Assemble the hamburgers, alternating all the ingredients:
hamburger, speck, egg, onion, cucumber, tomatoes.

Drink with: a quality beer, icy cold

HOT DOG

For 6 hot dogs
Preparation time 5 minutes
Cooking time 10 minutes over gentle heat on the hot plate

4 brown onions
2 tablespoons olive oil
1 teaspoon cumin
3 tablespoons ketchup
6 hot dog buns
6 lovely knack sausages (frankfurts or hot dogs)

Peel the onions, slice them thinly. Gently sauté them in olive oil on the hot plate until they're lightly brown, then add the cumin, tomato sauce and allow to caramelize.
Grill the sausages and bread on the barbecue grill. Spread the caramelized onions on the buns, place the sausages on top, cover with the other half of the bun. Watch out for falling onions!

BREAKFAST

For 6 breakfasts
Preparation time 10 minutes
Cooking time 10 minutes on the hot plate

3 sweet onions
6 slices of bacon
1 bunch cilantro
6 eggs
6 English muffins
HP sauce (preferably classic woodsmoke flavor)

Peel and slice the onions, cook them on the hot plate with the bacon, add the leaves from the bunch cilantro.
Cook the eggs on the hotplate. Toast the muffins, spread them with HP sauce, assemble the sandwich with layers of bacon, egg, cilantro, onions.

TURKISH KEBAB

For 6 kebabs
Preparation time 15 minutes
Cooking time 15 minutes on the hotplate

1 lb 5 oz lamb shoulder
6 Turkish bread rolls
2 sweet white onions
1 iceberg lettuce
salt and pepper
Sauce:
3 tablespoons créme fraiche
    or Greek yogurt
1 tablespoon harissa

Cut the lamb shoulder into thin slices. Cook the lamb on the hot plate until it is well browned, and season. Brown the rolls in the fat from the lamb. Peel the onions, shred the lettuce.
For the sauce, combine the créme fraiche and harissa.
Spread the buns with the créme fraiche-harissa sauce.
Combine the lamb with the lettuce and onions.
Top the buns with this mixture. Serve immediately.

CHORIZO OMELETTE

For 6 sandwichs
Preparation time 15 minutes
Cooking time 10 minutes on the hotplate

2 baguettes
1 garlic clove
olive oil
2 tomatoes
2 French shallots
12 eggs
salt and pepper
baby shiso leaves (purple mint/perilla)
12 slices chorizo sausage

Cut each baguette into three sections, split and rub them with garlic and drizzle with a little olive oil. Seed the tomatoes and dice the flesh. Peel and finely chop the French shallots.
Beat the eggs with a fork, add the French shallots and tomatoes, season. Cook 6 omelettes on the hotplate, add the shiso leaves.
Brown the slices of chorizo, then brown the bread in the fat from the chorizo. Place one omelette in each section of baguette and top it with two slices chorizo.

Drink with: beer again (there's some left over…)

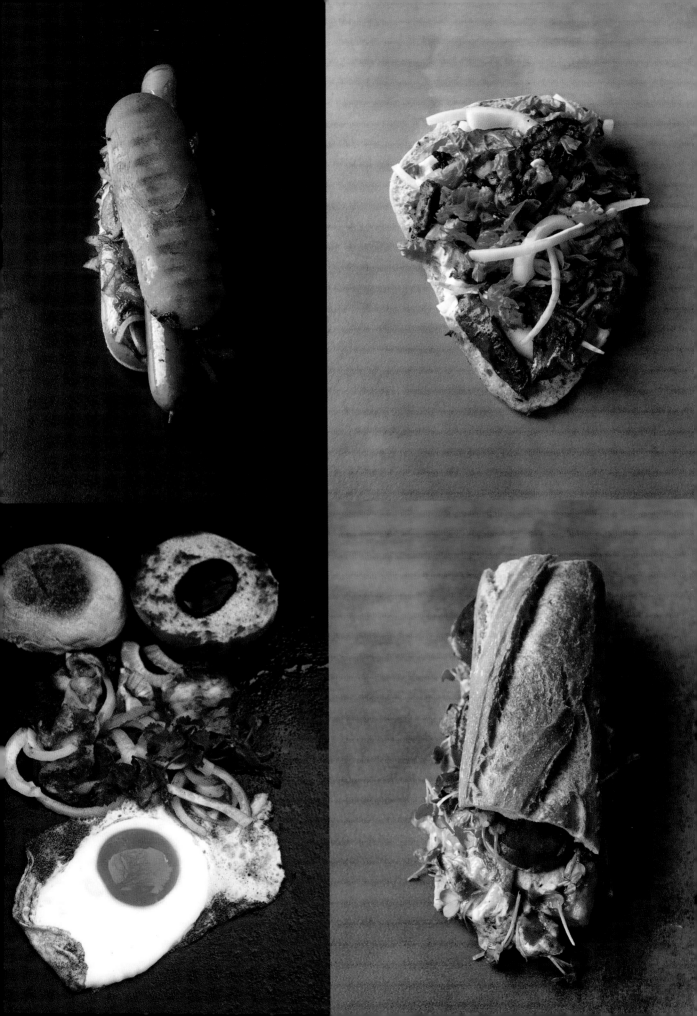

VEGETARIAN BURGERS

With ultra-cooooool people

Serves 6
Preparation time 15 minutes
Cooking time 10 minutes on the hot plate

12 spears green asparagus
2 red onions
1 fennel bulb
3 green tomatoes
3 tablespoons crème fraîche
1 tablespoon tomato paste
6 soy burger patties
1 cup finely grated parmesan cheese
6 hamburger buns
1 handful arugula
olive oil
salt and pepper

Cut the spears of asparagus in two lengthways, then into four
sections. Peel the onions, and slice them thinly along with the
fennel. Slice the green tomatoes into rounds.
Combine the crème fraîche with the tomato paste.
Cook the asparagus, red onions and fennel on the hotplate.
Make small mounds of parmesan cheese and brown to make
crisps. Cook the soy burgers. Brown the hamburger buns.
Dress the arugula with olive oil, season with salt and pepper.
Spread the buns with the crème fraîche-tomato paste mixture.
Assemble with layers of each ingredient: asparagus, soy burger,
parmesan, red onions, fennel, tomatoes, arugula.

Drink with: a greeeeen tea

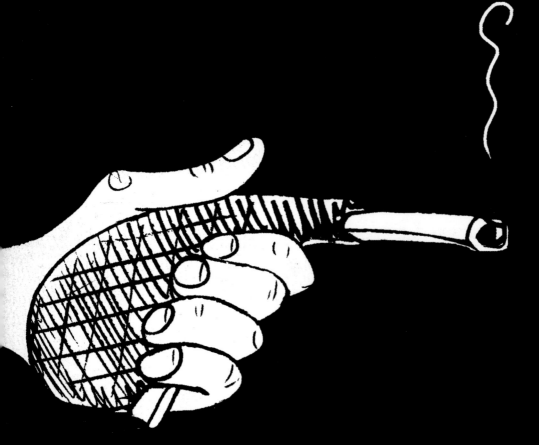

CHAPTER IV

RIBS
&
CUT
LETS

THE LEGEND: BEEF RIB CUTLET

The beef rib cutlet (rib eye/côte de bœuf) is synonymous with barbecue, the one is unimaginable without the other. Some have even wondered whether barbecue exists because of the beef rib cutlet, or if it's the other way around. They go together, but we will never know which came first. The beef rib cutlet is a stand-out dish which deserves special attention both when you choose the meat and when you cook it. The first stage is choosing your rib eye. It is wise to go to a butcher who will cut it in front of you—you can then choose the thickness according to the number of carnivores in your party; it should, as a minimum, weigh more than 2 lb 4 oz. The bone must be whole, never buy a rib whose bone has been cut in the middle, it won't have that extra bit of fat on the side, which provides that extra bit of gustatory pleasure so dear to our palate.

The beef needs to be aged to bring out its full taste and tenderness. Choose high quality beef to ensure good marbling, color and flavor.

THE BEEF RIB CUTLET

With no one, I'm eating it all by myself, end of story!

Serves 1
Preparation time 5 minutes
Cooking time 20 minutes

1 beef rib cutlet (rib eye) weighing 2 lb 10 oz
sea salt

Light the coals, cook the beef 10 minutes each side, enjoy
at your leisure.

The cooking of the beef rib cutlet is of prime importance for
the perfect eating experience. It should be seared over high
heat to create a caramelized crust all over. This crust allows
you to imprison the juices inside the beef (allow 20 minutes
to cook a 2 lb 6 oz rib rare). It should rest for a few minutes
before being sacrificed to the raging hunger of that day's guests.
A beef rub cutlet on a barbecue makes the ferocious appetite all
the keener. Make sure you have enough or risk a group sulk!
Serve with the sea salt.

Drink with: none of your business

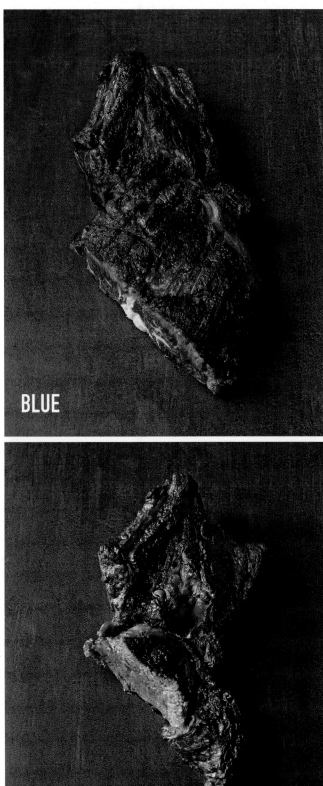

BLUE

WELL DONE

MEDIUM

RARE

FAR WEST RIBS

With a cowboy

Serves 6
Preparation time 10 minutes
Marinating time 12 hours
Cooking time 45 minutes in boiling water
+ 20 minutes over gentle heat

2 lb 10 oz pork spareribs
Marinade:
4 onions
6 garlic cloves
2 tablespoons herbes de Provençe (usually
  marjoram, oregano, rosemary, thyme)
1 tablespoon tomato paste
½ cup white wine
6 tablespoons ketchup
2 tablespoons HP sauce (preferably classic
  woodsmoke flavor)
2 tablespoons soy sauce
2 tablespoons Maggi seasoning sauce
1 tablespoon coarsely ground black pepper

Cook the spareribs for 45 minutes in gently simmering water.
For the marinade, peel the onions and garlic and finely chop
them. Combine all of the marinade ingredients. Reserve some
marinade for serving. Cover the spareribs with the remainder
of the marinade and chill for 12 hours.
Arrange the ribs over gentle heat, allow them to caramelize
at their leisure turning them regularly. Roll them in reserved
marinade before serving.

Drink with: brisk acidic rosé with intense fruitiness

RIBS & CUTLETS

PORK CHOP WITH HERBS

With a dietitian (pork is good, not fatty!)

Serves 6
Preparation time 15 minutes
Cooking time 20 minutes over gentle heat

6 pork chops
Herb salad:
1 bunch chervil
1 bunch cilantro
½ bunch mint
2 lemons
3 bulb spring onions
3 tablespoons olive oil
salt and pepper

Cook the pork chops over gentle heat for 10 minutes each side: they should be well browned.
For the salad, pick the leaves from the bunches of herbs, keep them in the refrigerator. Juice and zest the lemons. Slice the bulb spring onions. Combine the herbs with the bulb spring onions, drizzle with olive oil, add the lemon zest and juice and season.
Serve the pork chops topped with the herb salad.

Drink with: sparkling mineral water (to please the dietitian)

PORK STEAKS & WHOLEGRAIN MUSTARD

With gusto

Serves 6
Preparation time 15 minutes
Cooking time 20 minutes over gentle heat

6 pork neck steaks (or pork scotch fillet)
Mustard crust:
2 egg whites
6 tablespoons wholegrain mustard
1 tablespoon herbes de Provençe (usually marjoram, oregano, rosemary, thyme)
salt and pepper

First make the mustard crust. Whisk the egg whites with a fork, add the wholegrain mustard and herbes de Provençe and season. Spread the chops with the egg white-mustard mixture, cook over gentle heat and on a clean barbecue grill for 20 minutes. Important: the less you turn your chops, the more the mustard crust will stay on the meat.

Drink with good Grappa that lets you taste the soil and sun

EMMANUEL'S SPECIAL CUTLETS

With Emmanuel

Serves 6
Preparation time 10 minutes
Marinating time 3 hours
Cooking time 10 minutes over high heat

18 lamb cutlets
6 bulb spring onions
salt and pepper
Cider marinade:
8 garlic cloves
⅔ cup olive oil
¾ cup dry cider
1 tablespoon dried thyme
1 tablespoon dried rosemary

First make the marinade. Peel and crush the garlic. Gently brown the garlic in the olive oil. Combine with the cider, add the thyme and rosemary. Marinate the cutlets in the olive oil-cider mixture for 3 hours. Halve the bulb spring onions lengthways. Barbecue the cutlets with the onions over high heat, 1–2 minutes on each side (they should be well browned on the outside and juicy on the inside), season.

Drink with: dry cider

RACK OF LAMB WITH TAPENADE

With your partner's friends (that way you can stay beside the barbecue 'sorry not to be sitting down with you [yippee!], but I have to watch the food', without revealing the little interest you have in the dinner that's been imposed on you!)

Serves 6
Preparation time 15 minutes
Cooking time 20 minutes over gentle heat

3 racks of lamb
spicy salt (see page 18)
Tapenade:
7 oz Kalamata olives
1 oxheart tomato
1 bunch rosemary
2 garlic cloves
6 anchovies in oil
⅔ cup olive oil
3 tablespoons cognac
1 bunch fresh thyme

Rub the racks of lamb with the spicy salt, cook them over gentle heat for about 20 minutes, making sure you turn them regularly. The fat dripping from the racks can catch alight, so you have to stay by the barbecue to watch over them.
Separate the chops and top with tapenade.
For the tapenade, pit the olives. Cut the tomato into ½ inch thick slices. Place the tomato slices on the barbecue, burn the rosemary under the tomatoes, grill them 2 minutes each side. Dice the grilled tomatoes. Roughly process the olives with the garlic, anchovies, cognac and olive oil, add the diced tomato and the leaves picked from the bunch of thyme.

Drink with: truly great red—magnum bottle (you need some compensation, after all!)

VEAL CHOPS WITH SHALLOT BUTTER

With your GOOD blood test results. That's right, I have no cholesterol!

Serves 6
Preparation time 15 minutes
Cooking time 10 to 15 minutes over high heat

3 thick veal chops
Shallot butter:
1 garlic clove
2 French shallots
1 bunch chives
5½ oz lightly salted butter
1 teaspoon coarsely ground black pepper

For the butter, peel and finely chop the garlic and French shallots. Snip the chives into small sections. Using a fork, work the butter until it is soft and incorporate the garlic, pepper, French shallots and chives. Keep the butter at room temperature.
Cook the veal chops over high heat for 10–15 minutes (according to thickness and how you like it cooked).
Spread generously with the shallot butter, serve immediately.

Drink with: Burgundian-style red with a torrent of fruit (magnum bottle). That's right, no triglycerides either!

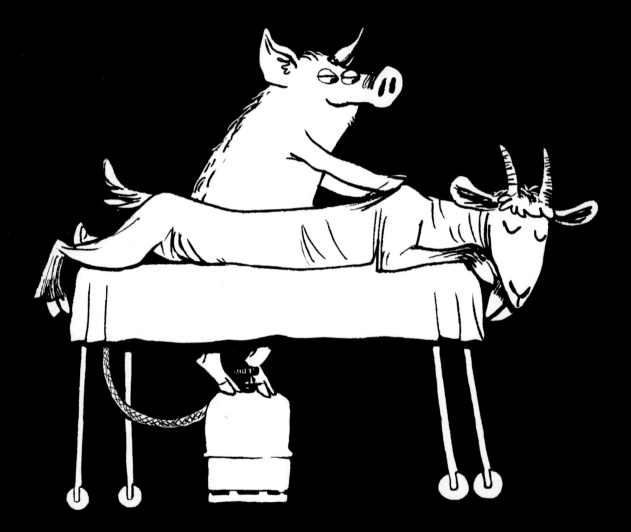

CHAPTER V

BAR
BE
CUE
XXL

WHOLE ROASTS

Whole roasts are to the barbecue what three Michelin stars are to gastronomy: a must.

In summer, there's always something to celebrate. The barbecue will then show its XXL face. No more individual skewers, you throw yourself into large-scale catering, you plan big.

If you're talking whole roasts, you're talking slow cooking, and everything this implies in terms of preparation. The night before, you dig a hole to make a home for your half-barrel, you put your load of wood inside, an old newspaper and a box of matches.

You make a marinade: olive oil, white wine, herbs, mustard which will refresh the beast throughout the long cooking and give it the desired flavors.

On the day, you get up early (5 or 6 in the morning, prior to the commencement of hostilities) to prepare the embers. The cooking needs to be gentle to obtain a crisp skin and well-cooked, juicy meat inside. Cooking time depends on the size of the piece being cooked, patience is the order of the day. You need arms willing and able to turn a spit: allow a quantity of chilled rosé to motivate the troops. This even, regular cooking is the key to the success of your roasted lamb, pig or any other animal.

The cooking is finished, the knives are sharpened, jaws are clenched ready for battle. The carving starts, plates jostle, congratulations ring out on all sides, it certainly deserves 'three stars'!

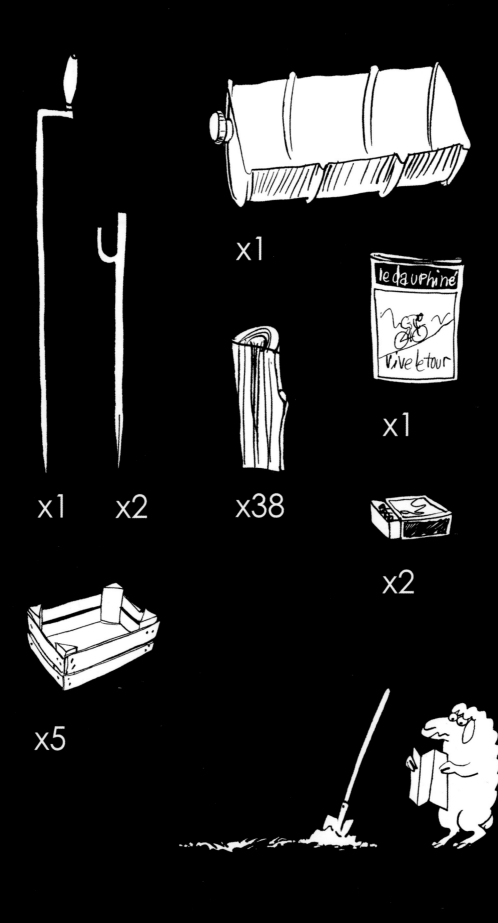

'TOADED' CHICKEN WITH MUSTARD

With a prince charming

Serves 6
Preparation time 20 minutes
Marinating time 24 hours
Cooking time 45 minutes over gentle heat

1 beautiful free-range chicken
salt and pepper
1 bunch flat-leafed parsley
1 bunch scallions
Marinade:
6 garlic cloves
4 tablespoons dijon mustard
1 tablespoon honey
1 teaspoon dried oregano
2 tablespoons olive oil

Cut open the breast side of the chicken and flatten it out
by pressing down hard (it will then look like a large toad).
For the marinade, peel and chop the garlic. Combine all
of the marinade ingredients: garlic, mustard, honey, oregano,
olive oil.
Lay the chicken down in a dish, spread over this marinade
(on both sides), season, cover with plastic wrap, chill for
24 hours.
Place the chicken over gentle heat, and cook it for 45 minutes,
turning from time to time. Once the chicken is cooked,
scatter with chopped parsley and scallions and cover for
2 minutes so they soften. Serve immediately.

Drink with: any princely wine

CAJUN-STYLE CHICKEN

With a banjo player

Serves 6
Preparation time 20 minutes
Marinating time 24 hours
Cooking time 1 hour over gentle heat, covered

1 beautiful free-range chicken
1 small soft cheese (such as Boursin or cream
  cheese flavored with herbs and garlic)
Marinade:
8 garlic cloves
2 tablespoons ground piment d'Espelette
  (or hot paprika)
2 tablespoons herbes de Provençe (usually
  marjoram, oregano, rosemary, thyme)
2 tablespoons paprika
4 tablespoons olive oil
juice of one lemon
salt and pepper

For the marinade, peel and slice the garlic. Combine with the
piment d'Espelette, herbes de Provençe, paprika, olive oil and
lemon juice, season.
Combine the Boursin cheese with 2 spoonfuls of this marinade
and place inside the chicken. Massage the chicken with the rest
of the marinade, rubbing it in well. Keep in the refrigerator for
24 hours.
Cook the chicken over gentle heat, covered, for 1 hour, turning
it from time to time. Cut up the chicken and dress it with the
cheese that has melted during cooking.

Drink with: fresh light red with a distinct violet aroma

SPIT-ROASTED SUCKLING PIG

**With the whole family as long as it's a large one.
Set the alarm for 5 am to prepare the embers.**

Serves 20+
Preparation time 30 minutes
Cooking time 3 hours over gentle heat

1 suckling pig, weighing approx 40 lb
Marinade:
30 garlic cloves
10 onions
6 dried chilis
6 bay leaves
1 lb 2 oz dijon mustard
4 cups olive oil
1 bottle white wine
Stuffing:
6 onions
8 carrots
8 granny smith apples
8 average slices brioche
4 cups crème fraîche
4 lb 8 oz sausage meat
1 tablespoon juniper berries
2 branches rosemary
2 sprigs fresh thyme
2 bay leaves
⅔ cup cognac
salt and pepper

To make the marinade, peel the garlic and onions. Chop them
up finely with the chilies and bay leaves, combine with the
mustard, olive oil and white wine.
For the stuffing, peel the onions, carrots and apples. Slice the
onions and cut the carrots and apples into segments. Cut the
brioche into cubes and soak in the crème fraîche. Combine
all the stuffing ingredients together, mixing well, and season.
Stuff the pig with this mixture, sew up the belly with metal
thread. Place the pig on the spit, wrap the ears in foil. Tie
together the back legs and front legs.
Place the pig over gentle heat for 3 hours, basting regularly
with marinade (make sure you have some wood coal handy in
case the embers from the morning are not enough). It needs to
cook slowly and gently so the skin can caramelize at its leisure
while the meat cooks in peace. Ask your favorite uncle to lend
you a hand carving the pig.

**Drink with: the little red that your uncle Jack brought
back in the 20-liter cask from his trip to the vineyards**

SPIT-ROASTED LAMB

With all your friends…the ones who could be bothered with the trip…Same wake-up time as for the pig, there's no helping it!

Serves 20
Preparation time 45 minutes
Cooking time 3 hours over gentle heat

1 lamb, weighing 33 lb
Arugula Marinade:
1 bunch arugula
2 cups olive oil
2 cups white port
juice of 2 lemons
6 garlic cloves, peeled
salt and pepper
Pesto:
6 bunches basil
4 cups olive oil
7 oz parmesan cheese
3 French shallots, peeled
⅔ cup pine nuts
2 garlic cloves, peeled
salt and pepper
Chili Marinade:
5 bird's eye chilis
1 tablespoon tomato paste
6 tablespoons brown sugar
juice of 3 lemons
6 garlic cloves, peeled
2 cups sunflower oil
¾ cup rice vinegar
¾ cup pineapple juice
salt and pepper
Tomato Marinade:
14 oz sundried tomatoes in oil
4 tablespoons ketchup
1 tablespoon dried thyme
1 small can anchovies in oil
3 cups olive oil
salt and pepper

Lamb meat is tender and delicate. Spit roasted lamb, using woodfire cooking, will take the flavor to a new level. Put the lamb on the spit with its front and hind legs attached to the spit. Cook for a leisurely 3 hours, regularly massaging it with your choice of marinade.
To make the marinades and pesto, process all the ingredients for each together and let the guests choose. Reserve some of each for serving and use the rest for basting.

Drink with: the little rosé that Nick brought back in a 10-liter cask (he's not as strong as uncle Jack!!) from his neck of the woods

CHAPTER VI

HIGH
&
LOW
TIDE

REELY GOOD...

Saturday arrives with a sun capable of tanning hides in under 2 minutes and your sandals (size 11 if you please) wait impatiently beside the door. You're going camping. Summer was crying out to 'hit the road', the trunk is overflowing with baggage, the roofrack is fully loaded. You're packed like sardines in the car, a fishing rod between your toes, but it doesn't matter, you're happy. Happy to be facing 12 hours in the car, happy to imagine the future barbecues at nightfall.

It's been a week now since the tent was put up, a week since the rod was set up, a week with nothing on the barbecue but sausages...It is high time you realized that the fish shop is the best fishing spot. Red mullet, bass, john dory, mackerels and sardines are all there thumbing their noses at us, a reminder of the hours spent on the rocks dreaming of such miracles. It's game on for a fish grill.

You use good hot coals to caramelize the skin while keeping the inside juicy. The cooking needs to be quick and well controlled, the barbecue gets its summer sheen back, it's time for champagne!

BASS WITH FENNEL

With fishing friends (to show off!)

Serves 6
Preparation time 20 minutes
Cooking time 30 minutes over high heat

2 sea bass, each weighing 2 lb 10 oz
2 tablespoons fennel seeds
few stalks of wild fennel or
   1 bunch dill
sea salt
Marinade:
3 tomatoes
1 scallion
1 bunch chives
1 basket red currants (or cranberries)
2 tablespoons light soy sauce
¾ cup olive oil

Clean and gut the bass, remove the gills, fill the cavity with
the fennel seeds and wild fennel.
For the marinade, plunge the tomatoes in boiling water for
10 seconds, remove the skin. Dice the flesh. Finely chop the
scallion, chop the chives, pick the red currants off the bunch.
Combine all the marinade ingredients with the soy sauce and
olive oil.
Cook the bass for 15 minutes on each side (wait for the the
first side to be well browned before turning the fish, or the
skin will stick to the grill). Remove the fish, drizzle with
marinade, season with sea salt.

**Drink with: organic chablis at slightly colder than cellar
temperature**

BLACK SEABREAM

With our new friends

Serves 6
Preparation time 15 minutes
Cooking time 20 minutes over high heat

3 black seabream, each weighing 14 oz
sea salt
¾ cup olive oil
Stuffing:
2¾ oz Kalamata olives
4 bulb spring onions
3 beautiful very ripe tomatoes
2 sprigs lemon thyme

Brush the cleaned bream with some of the olive oil.
For the stuffing, pit the olives, and roughly chop them.
Finely slice the bulb spring onions, finely dice the tomatoes,
pick the leaves from the thyme, combine everything.
Stuff the bream with a third of this mixture. Season the fish
with sea salt. Combine the rest of the stuffing mixture with
the remainder of the olive oil to make a marinade and set
aside. Barbecue the bream over high heat, 10 minutes each
side (the point of a knife should easily reach the backbone).
Remove the fillets and coat with marinade.

Drink with: crisp clean sauvignon blanc

JOHN DORY

With your religious friends

Serves 6
Preparation time 15 minutes
Cooking time 20 minutes over high heat

3 beautiful john dory (see Note)
Shallot-tomato compote:
2 fresh tomatoes
2 French shallots
1 glass dry white wine (approx ½ cup)
1 tablespoon brown sugar
3½ oz sundried tomatoes in oil
salt and pepper
1 bunch fresh thyme

Cut the head off each fish, Amen.
For the compote, plunge the fresh tomatoes into boiling water
for 30 seconds and peel them. Seed the tomatoes and keep the
flesh. Peel and slice the French shallots, cook them over a low
heat in a saucepan in the white wine with the sugar. Add the
sundried tomatoes and the fresh tomatoes and cook until you
have a thick compote. Season, add the leaves of the fresh thyme.
Cook the fish over high heat for 10 minutes each side. Remove
and serve with the compote.

Note: An alternative fish option to john dory would be grouper,
snapper, halibut, cod, or sea bass.

Drink with: communion wine

MACKEREL WITH LEMON

With people you don't want to be seen with

Serves 6
Preparation time 20 minutes
Cooking time 10 minutes over high heat

6 mackerels
sea salt
Lemon marinade:
3 eggs
3 lemons
1¾ oz caperberries
¾ cup olive oil

Clean the mackerel.
For the marinade, boil the eggs for 10 minutes, run them
under cold water, peel and roughly chop them. Zest two of the
lemons, take out the segments of all three lemons, removing all
skin and pith. Slice the caperberries, combine all the ingredients
with the olive oil.
Cook the mackerel 5 minutes each side. Remove the fish
and drizzle with the marinade and season with sea salt.

**Drink with: light green gold sauvignon blanc with a nose
of celery, unripe apples and blackboard chalk**

SARDINES

With the neighbors—avoiding the problem of the smell

Serves 6
Preparation time 15 minutes
Cooking time 5 minutes over high heat

24 very fresh sardines
2 baguettes
sea salt
Herb-garlic olive oil:
6 garlic cloves
⅔ cup olive oil
1 tablespoon herbes de Provençe (usually
   marjoram, oregano, rosemary, thyme)

Purists do not gut sardines, the rest do.
For the herb-garlic mixture, peel the garlic, and slice it thinly.
Gently heat the olive oil, add the garlic until it takes on a
golden brown color, then add the herbes de Provençe.
Grill slices of baguette on the barbecue. Cook the sardines
over high heat 2–3 minutes each side and take out the fillets
(with your fingers).
Dip the grilled bread in the garlic olive oil, arrange the sardine
fillets on top and sprinkle with sea salt.

Drink with: whatever the neighbors brought

RED MULLET LIVER TOASTS

With a passionate fisherman

Serves 6
Preparation time 20 minutes
Cooking time 10 minutes over high heat and on the hot plate

6 beautiful red mullets
6 slices baguette
3 sprigs dried thyme
12 pickling onions
12 Kalamata olives
1 bunch flat-leafed parsley
½ cup olive oil
salt and pepper

Clean the red mullet, taking care to reserve the liver, rinse
the fish and add the dried thyme. Peel and slice the pickling
onions, pit and slice the olives, pick the leaves from the parsley.
Sauté these ingredients with the liver on the hotplate in a
little olive oil, season.
Drizzle the slices of baguette with olive oil, grill them on
the barbecue. Top them with the liver-onion-olive mixture.
Barbecue the mullet over high heat 5 minutes each side.
Serve with the toast.

**Drink with: red wine for the red mullet—a nutty wine
showing crushed almonds, hazelnuts and macadamia on
top of cranberry and figs**

ANCHOVIES ON TOAST

With whoever drops in for drinks

Serves 6
Preparation time 10 minutes
Cooking time 5 minutes over high heat and on the hot plate

1 baguette
2 garlic cloves
¾ cup olive oil
6 bulb spring onions
3 ripe tomatoes
12 fresh anchovies
sea salt and pepper

Slice the baguette lengthways to make large toasts. Peel the
garlic, rub over the bread. Drizzle each slice with some olive oil.
Slice the bulb spring onions, cut the tomatoes into segments.
Sauté the tomatoes and onions on the hotplate in a little
olive oil.
Barbecue the whole anchovies 2 minutes over high heat, remove
the fillets with your fingers and grill the slices of baguette on the
barbecue.
Top each slice with the tomato-onion mixture, arrange the
anchovy fillets on top, season with sea salt and pepper.

Drink with: smooth and fruity white with stony citrus nose

CUTTLEFISH

With Loïc Perron or any other famous sailor you know

Serves 6
Preparation time 15 minutes
Cooking time 5 minutes over high heat

6 cleaned cuttlefish
salt and pepper
Marinade:
2 lemongrass stems
2 scallions
1 bunch dill
⅔ cup olive oil
1 teaspoon brown sugar
juice of 1 lemon
1 teaspoon curry powder
1 tablespoon fish sauce

Using a utility knife or box cutter (with the blade extended to half the thickness of the cuttlefish), slash the outside (rounded side) of the cuttlefish in a criss-cross pattern.
For the marinade, finely slice the lemongrass and scallions, pick the leaves from the dill. Combine these ingredients with the olive oil, sugar, lemon juice, curry powder and fish sauce. Barbecue the cuttlefish, slashed side down, for 3 minutes, then 2 minutes on the other side. Warning: cuttlefish cooks quickly and becomes tough when overcooked. Drizzle the cuttlefish with the marinade, season.

Drink with: summer quaffing white revealing honeysuckle and plenty of fruit

SHALLOT–LIME YELLOWFIN TUNA

With a meat-lover (yes, that's right!)

Serves 6
Preparation time 15 minutes
Marinating time 24 hours
Cooking time 15 minutes over high heat

6 echalions (banana shallots or elongated
  French shallots)
6 fillets yellowfin tuna
sea salt
Marinade:
2 limes
¾ cup olive oil
1 teaspoon ground cardamom

For the marinade, zest and juice the limes and combine with the olive oil and cardamom. Reserve a little for serving. Marinate the tuna in the marinade for 24 hours.
Peel the echalions, cut them in half. Cook the echalions on the barbecue for 15 minutes. Drizzle the echalions with the reserved marinade, season with sea salt. Serve immediately with tuna.
Sear the tuna fillets according to how each person likes it cooked.

Drink with: varietal Viognier

SALMON SAUCE VERTE

With friends of your dieting husband

Serves 6
Preparation time 20 minutes
Cooking time 15 minutes over high heat

1 salmon fillet
Sauce verte:
2 eggs
1 tablespoon strong mustard
1 bunch basil, leaves pulled
1 tablespoon rice vinegar
juice of 1 lemon
¾ cup olive oil
salt and pepper

Remove the salmon bones using tweezers.
For the sauce verte, bring a saucepan of water to a boil, immerse the eggs for 5 minutes, refresh them under cold water and peel them. Process the eggs with the mustard, basil leaves, rice vinegar, lemon juice and olive oil, season.
Place the salmon skin-side down on a very hot barbecue grill, cook for 5 minutes, turn the salmon over and cook a further 5 minutes. Remove the skin and place it flesh-side down on the barbecue for 5 minutes. Serve the salmon fillet while the skin is still crispy. Serve the sauce verte separately.

Drink with: clean pumped up chardonnay

JUMBO SHRIMP WITH FENNEL

With someone you love, they're expensive!

Serves 6
Preparation time 10 minutes
Cooking time 5 minutes over high heat, covered

18 beautiful jumbo shrimp
2 tablespoons pastis (aniseed flavored liqueur)
1 bunch wild fennel
1 tablespoon fennel seeds
sea salt

Drizzle the shrimp with pastis, cook them on the barbecue for 3 minutes, covered. Place the fennel on top of the shrimp and cover again for 2 minutes.
Serve immediately, sprinkle with fennel seeds and season with sea salt.

Drink with: champagne, while you're at it

TARRAGON SQUID

With a Jules Verne enthusiast

Serves 6
Preparation time 20 minutes
Cooking time 10 minutes over high heat

6 beautiful squid, each weighing 7 oz
1 teaspoon ground paprika
olive oil
Stuffing:
1 bunch tarragon
2 French shallots
5½ oz shelled pistachios
2 slices soft white sandwich bread
⅔ cup cream
2 eggs
1¼ cups cooked rice
salt and pepper

Clean the squid, making sure you reserve the tentacles, and rinse them thoroughly.
For the stuffing, pick the leaves from the tarragon, finely chop the French shallots. Process together the tarragon, pistachios, bread, cream and eggs. Add the French shallots and rice, season. Stuff the squid with this mixture, reposition the tentacles and attach them to the base with a toothpick. Sprinkle with paprika. Cook 5 minutes over high heat on each side. Drizzle with some olive oil.

Drink with: white burgundy loaded with an assault of orange peel and honey

EXECUTED LOBSTER

With an executioner

Serves 6
Freezer time: 1 hour
Preparation time 15 minutes
Cooking time 10 minutes over high heat

6 live lobsters
Herb butter:
1 French shallot
2 garlic cloves
1 tablespoon olive oil
1 bunch tarragon
½ bunch curly-leaf parsley
3½ oz lightly salted butter
salt and pepper

Place the lobsters in the freezer for about 1 hour to render them unconscious.
For the herb butter, peel and finely chop the French shallot. Peel and chop the garlic. Soften the shallot and garlic gently in the olive oil. Pick the leaves from the tarragon and parsley, process them with the butter and softened garlic and shallot, season and keep at room temperature.
Remove the lobsters from the freezer. Hold the lobster with the head facing you, shell-side down. Using a sharp chef's knife, cut the lobster in two by inserting the knife where the head meets the tail. Split the head, then the tail.
Sear the lobsters on the barbecue grill, 7–8 minutes shell-side down, and 2 minutes flesh side down. Spread the flesh with the herb butter.

Drink with: chardonnay that steps up in intensity as you taste

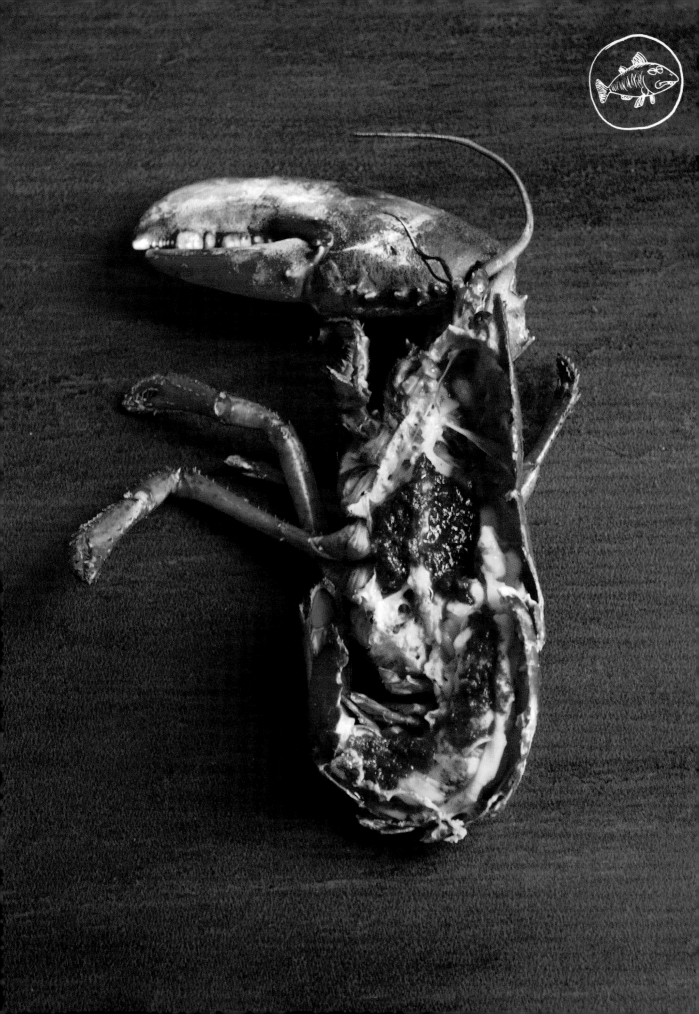

JUMBO SHRIMP AND SPRING VEGETABLES

With friends who didn't want to come – 'it's spring, we're watching what we eat'. I have just what you need.

Serves 6
Preparation time 20 minutes
Cooking time 5 minutes over high heat on the hot plate

18 beautiful jumbo shrimp
5½ oz snow peas
5½ oz green beans
12 spears of green asparagus
6 baby carrots
5½ oz podded broad beans
1 tablespoon butter
salt and pepper
Marinade:
2 garlic cloves
juice of one lemon
3 tablespoons soy sauce
1 tablespoon pastis (aniseed flavored liqueur)

Peel and devein the shrimp.
For the marinade, peel and crush the garlic, mix with the lemon juice, soy sauce and pastis. Drizzle the shrimp with this marinade. Reserve a little for deglazing.
Poach all the vegetables in boiling water and refresh them immediately. Melt the butter on the hot plate, add all of the vegetables, cook them 5 minutes and deglaze with the reserved shrimp marinade.
Barbecue the shrimp 2 minutes each side. Serve immediately with the vegetables.

Drink with: sparkling mineral water, to annoy the people who initially didn't want to come

SCALLOPS WITH GRILLED LETTUCE

With a lover or lovers

Serves 6
Preparation time 10 minutes
Cooking time 5 minutes over high heat

3 small heads romaine lettuce
1 tablespoon olive oil
12 scallops
6 thin slices speck (smoked ham or bacon)
Shallot vinaigrette:
3 French shallots
⅔ cup olive oil
1 tablespoon balsamic vinegar
1 teaspoon Savora mustard (or American mustard)

Remove the scallops from their shell and remove their roe.
For the vinaigrette, peel and finely slice the French shallots. Combine the shallots with the olive oil, balsamic vinegar and Savora mustard.
Halve the lettuces lengthways, brush them with olive oil. Barbecue the scallops 2 minutes each side (they should be almost raw in the middle). Barbecue the speck until it is crispy, sear the lettuces on the grill.
Arrange the scallops on a plate, add the lettuce, the speck (roughly sliced), and drizzle with the shallot vinaigrette.

Drink with: crisp, dry and invigorating muscadet or your favorite seafood wine

SCALLOPS AND SPECK

With pilgrims on the way to Bali

Serves 6
Preparation time 20 minutes
Cooking time 10 minutes on the hot plate

18 scallops
4 carrots
1 French shallot
2 garlic cloves
1 orange beet
6 slices speck (smoked ham or bacon)
1 bunch chives
2 tablespoons canola oil
salt and pepper

Remove the scallops from their shell and remove their roe.
Peel the carrots, cut them into ⅛ x ¼ inch sticks (julienne). Peel and finely chop the French shallot and the garlic. Peel the beet and cut it into thin julienne strips. Snip the chives into ¾ inch lengths. Slice the speck into strips.
Sauté the vegetables and the speck on the hot plate with the canola oil for 5 minutes. Sear the scallops 2–3 minutes each side. Add the chives to the vegetables, season.
Serve immediately.

Drink with: refined and delicate riesling

ROAST SALMON

With a seachanger

Serves 6
Preparation time 15 minutes
Cooking time 15 minutes over high heat

1 beautiful salmon fillet weighing about
  2 lb 10 oz, skin on
1 tablespoon fennel seeds
salt and pepper
oil
Seasoning:
2 French shallots
1 bunch cilantro
1 lemon
1 small bird's eye chili

Cut off the thin end of the salmon. Remove the bones using a pair of tweezers. Make an incision along the length of the salmon where the belly meets the loin, sliding the knife between the belly meat and the skin. Remove the belly meat (you could eat it tartare as an appetizer). You will then have a core of salmon meat with extra skin on the side.
For the seasoning, peel and finely chop the French shallots. Pick the leaves from the cilantro and roughly chop them. Zest the lemon. Chop up the bird's eye chili, removing the seeds.
Season the salmon loin with the seasoning and fennel seeds, season with salt and pepper. Roll the loin in its skin and tie it up with cooking twine soaked in salted water. Cook for 15 minutes in a little oil over high heat, turning the salmon at regular intervals. Serve in generous slices with the crispy skin.

Drink with: chardonnay, pure and simple

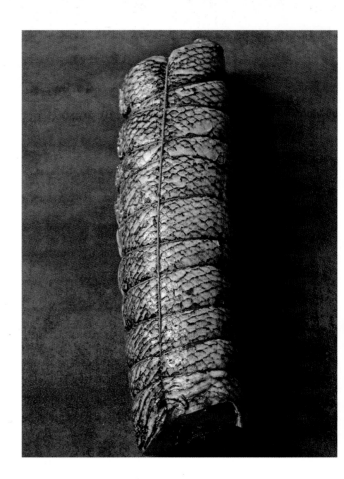

ROAST MONKFISH

With an avid hunter who's turning to fish

Serves 6
Preparation time 30 minutes
Cooking time 20 minutes over gentle heat, covered

2 monkfish tails, each weighing 1 lb 12 oz
  or any firm fleshed fish
18 thin slices of speck (smoked ham or bacon)
Sundried tomato purée:
1 bunch basil
1 garlic clove
¾ oz fresh ginger
1 orange
3½ oz sundried tomatoes in oil
salt and pepper

Separate the monkfish fillets from the central backbone.
Remove the thin membrane that covers the fillets.
For the purée, pick the leaves from the basil, peel the garlic and
ginger, juice and zest the orange. Process together the sun-dried
tomatoes, basil, orange zest, ginger and garlic. Loosen the purée
with the orange juice (it should have a smooth and creamy
texture), season.
Lay out the slices of speck, overlapping them slightly: the row
needs to be the same length as the monkfish. Lay a monkfish
fillet down with the thicker end towards you. Spread with
tomato purée, cover with another monkfish fillet (thick end
pointing the other way), roll in the speck.
Cook the monkfish over gentle heat (place the side where
the slices of speck 'join' down first). Cover, allow to cook for
10 minutes, then turn the roast over for a further 10 minutes.

Drink with: burgundy (or white for the purists)

SALMON ON FIR

With the vegetarians of the high plains

Serves 6
Preparation time 20 minutes
Cooking time 5 minutes over high heat, covered

1 salmon fillet
6 fir tree branches
salt and pepper
Marinade:
¾ cup olive oil
juice of 2 lemons
1 tablespoon miel de sapin (fir tree honey)

Remove the skin from the salmon fillet, remove the bones using
a pair of tweezers. Make thin slices of salmon, cutting from the
thicker end towards the tail.
For the marinade, combine the olive oil with the lemon juice,
add the honey.
Wrap the fir branches in slices of salmon, swaddling the
branches where the needles are and brush with marinade.
Place the fir on the barbecue, cover and cook for 5 minutes.
The salmon should stay pink in the center.
Serve the salmon on the fir branches and season.

Drink with: chenin blanc leaving the palate clean and dry

FINGER BURNERS

You weren't very good at line fishing, but we'll make up for it with some fishing by hand. Today we're preparing for a veritable shellfish hunt.

Knives, gloves, flippers, yabby pump nothing is left to chance. We need to forget the humiliation of the first week, when the by-word was 'empty-handed'! You spot a few well-watered rocks by the sea, to which mussels are clinging en masse. You divide the labor: one in the water to pick them from the bunch, one on the rock to collect and clean the booty, and you start to get back a little credibility.

Small holes with air bubbles in the wet sand suggest the hidden presence of cockles or pippies. He is a mistrustful creature, but with a quick shuffle with your toes, wham, you seize the beast, pluck him from his home, and wear a winner's grin.

When you're a Robinson Crusoe like an urban *Survivor*—guitar under the arm, bag of shellfish and dirty hair—you must be in for a special night of cooking. You light the fire, place that day's treasure on the flames and sing sea shanties in a true communion with Mother Nature.

SHELL
FISH
HUNT

RAZOR CLAMS WITH TARRAGON BUTTER

With a family that goes barefoot

Serves 6
Preparation time 10 minutes
Cooking time 5 minutes over high heat

36 fresh razor clams
Tarragon butter:
1 bunch tarragon
2 French shallots
5½ oz lightly salted butter

For the tarrogan butter, pick the leaves from the tarragon.
Peel and finely slice the French shallots, process the shallots
and tarragon with the butter.
Arrange the razor clams over the hot coals, flesh side down,
for 5 minutes until they take on a golden color.
Melt the tarragon butter in a saucepan and drizzle over the
razor clams. Swallow the razors, walk on the coals.

Drink with: an aromatic white (preferably from the Rhône)

THE GROUND-DWELLERS

Still with the same crowd

Serves 6
Preparation time 15 minutes
Cooking time 5 minutes

mussels
oysters
razor clams
hard-shell clams
other kinds of clam
and everything in the way of shellfish that
   the day's fishing trip has brought in

Make a cosy bed out of pine needles (like a country mattress that molds to your body, thick like a brioche fresh out of the oven). On this mattress arrange all kinds of shellfish, and light the fire like the Johnny Hallyday song: *"allumer le feu, allumer le feu, et faire danser les diables et les dieux, allumer le feu, allumer le feu, et voir grandir la flamme dans vos yeux, allumer le feu..."*
Enjoy sitting on the ground, bring the guitar out and *"allumer le feu, allumer le feu, et faire danser les diables et les dieux..."*.

Drink with: whatever's left at the bottom of the icebox, if indeed there is anything left

ÉCLADE

With passing friends

Serves 6
Preparation time 15 minutes
Cooking time 5 minutes

6 lb 12 oz mussels
dozens of pine needles that the
 children have gathered

Arrange the mussels in a large pan (like a paella pan), with
the pointed (hinge) end upwards—when the mussel opens,
it mustn't fill with ash. Cover generously with very dry pine
needles, shoo the children back to a safe distance, light the
needles, wait for the mussels to open.
Enjoy from the pan.

Drink with: the fruity white in the back of the fridge

CHAPTER VII

POTATOES IN EMBERS

Serves 6
Preparation time 15 minutes
Cooking time 30 minutes in slow coals

6 beautiful potatoes

Wrap the potatoes in foil. Place them right on the embers, cover with more embers for about 30 minutes. The potato needs to be soft to the touch.
Serve with the accompaniments below.

TARRAGON CREAM

1 bunch tarragon
1 French shallot
4 tablespoons Greek yogurt
2 tablespoons crème fraîche
salt and pepper

Pick the leaves from the bunch of tarragon and chop them finely. Peel and finely chop the French shallot. Combine everything with the yogurt and crème fraîche, season.

PISTACHIO PESTO

1 bunch basil
5½ oz pistachios
¾ cup olive oil
1¾ oz parmesan cheese
1 French shallot
salt and pepper

Pick the leaves from the basil. Process the pistachios, basil, olive oil and parmesan cheese, season. Peel and finely chop the French shallot, add it to the pistachio pesto.

SAUCE VIERGE

3 ripe tomatoes
1 bunch basil
2 bulb spring onions
1 tablespoon capers
¾ cup olive oil
salt and pepper

Plunge the tomatoes into boiling water for 30 seconds, remove the skin and finely dice the flesh. Pick the leaves from the basil and finely chop them, chop the bulb spring onions. Combine everything with the capers and olive oil, season.

SPICED TOMATOES

6 tomatoes
2 garlic cloves
1 onion
1 oz ginger
3 tablespoons olive oil
1 tablespoon soy sauce
salt and pepper

Plunge the tomatoes into boiling water for 30 seconds, remove the skin and finely dice the flesh. Peel and chop the garlic, onion and ginger. Gently sauté this mixture in the olive oil, add the diced tomato and allow to stew together.
Process everything together, add the soy sauce, season.

ONIONS
WITH PEPPER BUTTER

Serves 6
Preparation time 5 minutes
Cooking time 15 minutes over gentle heat

6 beautiful brown onions
4¼ oz lightly salted butter
1 teaspoon sichuan peppercorns
1 teaspoon coarsely ground black pepper

Cut a cross in the top of the onions, cutting two thirds of
the way down. Place ¾ oz butter inside each onion, season with
a combination of peppers.
Wrap the onions in foil, place them directly on the embers,
cover them with more embers (cross facing upwards)
for 15 minutes. The onions should be soft to the touch.
Serve with barbecued fish or offal—the acidic note of
the onions goes well with them.

YOUNG GARLIC

Serves 6
Preparation time 5 minutes
Cooking time 15 minutes over gentle heat

3 heads of garlic
2¼ oz lightly salted butter
1 tablespoon herbes de Provençe (usually
   marjoram, oregano, rosemary, thyme)
1 sprig fresh thyme

Slice the top off the heads of garlic. Place a pat of butter on
each head, scatter with herbes de Provençe and fresh thyme
leaves. Place the top back on the garlic.
Wrap each head of garlic in foil. Place over gentle heat for
15 minutes. Serve alongside barbecued meat.

TOMATOES WITH LEMON THYME

Serves 6
Preparation time 10 minutes
Cooking time 5 minutes over high heat

12 black krim tomatoes (or other large heirloom tomatoes)
6 French shallots
½ cup olive oil
1 bunch lemon thyme
sea salt

Remove the tomato stems and cut the tomatoes in half. Peel the French shallots and cut them in half. On a barbecue grill that's been oiled and is nice and hot, arrange the tomatoes and shallots, cover with lemon thyme. Cover with a cloche (see note) and cook for 5 minutes. Serve drizzled with some olive oil, season with seal salt.

Note: You can make a bell-shaped cover from foil.

PEPPERS + CHORIZO

Serves 6
Preparation time 30 minutes
Cooking time 15 minutes over high heat and on the hotplate

2 red peppers
2 green peppers
2 yellow peppers
6 garlic cloves
5½ oz spicy chorizo sausage
⅔ cup olive oil
salt and pepper

Barbecue the peppers whole over high heat, until their skin blackens and puffs up. Seal them inside a plastic bag for 20 minutes. Remove the skin and cut the peppers into strips. Peel and finely slice the garlic cloves. Julienne the chorizo sausage. Sauté the chorizo and garlic on the hot plate in the olive oil, top the peppers with this mixture, add a drizzle of olive oil, season.
This mixture keeps for one week, covered with olive oil.
These peppers are the perfect accompaniment to barbecued meats such as a lamb dish.

CORN

Serves 6
Preparation time 5 minutes
Cooking time 5 minutes in simmering water + 5 minutes over gentle heat

6 fresh young corn cobs
3½ oz lightly salted butter
1 tablespoon ground piment d'Espelette (or hot paprika)
salt and pepper

Strip the husks off the corn cobs. Plunge them into boiling water and cook them for 5 minutes at a bare simmer. Melt half of the butter. Brush the corn with the butter and cook them over gentle heat for 5 minutes, turning them regularly. Serve speared on 2 picks, sprinkle over a little piment d'Espelette, add a pat of butter, season.

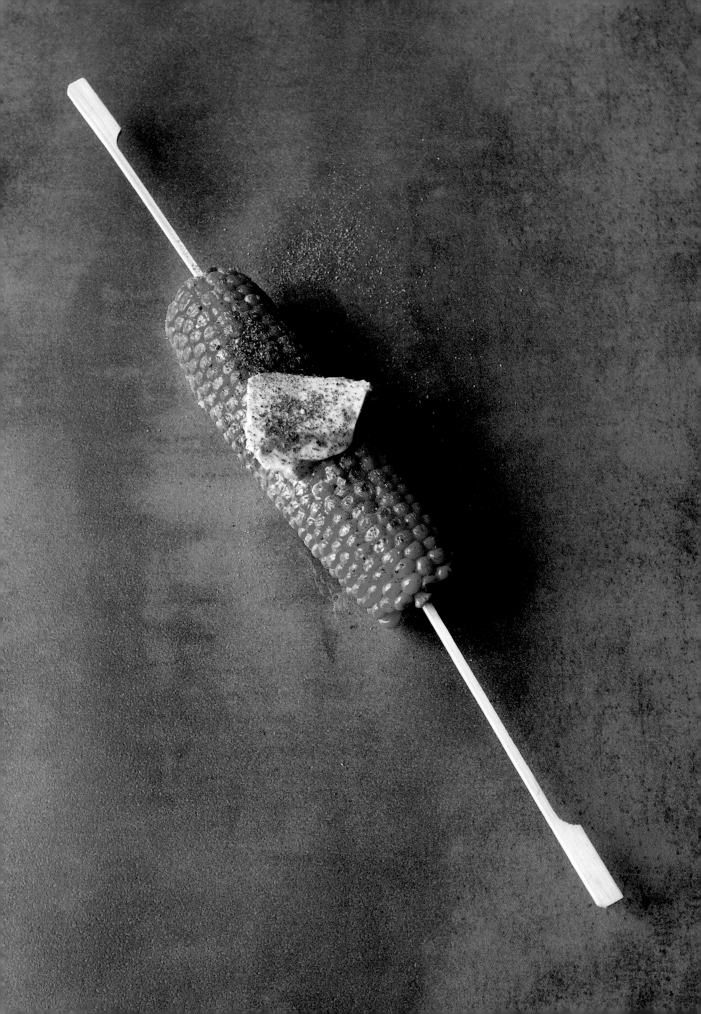

VEGETABLES GRILLED WITH MINT

Serves 6
Preparation time 20 minutes
Cooking time 10 minutes on the hot plate

12 spears of green asparagus
1 bunch mint
12 mild green chilies
12 mild red chilies
12 cherry tomatoes
1⅓ cups fresh peas
½ cup fresh broad beans
2 tablespoons olive oil
salt and pepper

Cut the asparagus spears in half lengthways, then into two sections. pick the leaves from the mint. Remove the seeds from the chilies.
On a hot plate that's nice and hot, sauté all the vegetables in the olive oil to sear them (they should stay firm). Add the mint at the end, season.

GRILLED CEP MUSHROOMS

Serves 6
Preparation time 10 minutes + 1 day to find them
Cooking time 5 minutes over high heat

12 small cep mushrooms ('champagne
  cork' or bouchon)
⅔ cup olive oil
sea salt and pepper

When the basket is overflowing with cep mushrooms, when the legs are heavy, when the call of the table is felt in the belly and the fangs sharpen, then it is high time to head home and show off the day's pickings.
Scrape the mushrooms with a knife and wipe them. Cut them in half. Pour the olive oil into a small dish. Briefly dip the mushrooms in the oil, cut-side down, sear them over high heat 2 minutes on the cut side and 2 minutes on the outside. Season with sea salt and pepper.

EGGPLANT GRILLED WITH SAGE

With girls

Serves 6
Preparation time 15 minutes
Cooking time 10 minutes over gentle heat

12 sage leaves, reserve a few for garnish
⅔ cup olive oil
2 lovely eggplants
sea salt

The night before, process the sage leaves with the olive oil, leave at room temperature. Slice the eggplants into rounds ¼ inch thick. Drizzle the slices of eggplant with the sage oil. The next day, barbecue the eggplant slices until soft, marking them with a criss-cross grill pattern. Season with sea salt, and garnish with a few sage leaves.

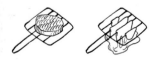

RATATOUILLE PARCELS

With different girls

Serves 6
Preparation time 15 minutes
Cooking time 15 minutes over gentle heat

2 beautiful eggplants
2 red peppers
2 yellow peppers
4 bulb spring onions
1¾ oz fresh ginger
1 organic lemon (unwaxed)
⅔ cup olive oil
½ cup white port
1 branch rosemary
1 bay leaf
salt and pepper

Finely dice the vegetables. Peel and finely slice the ginger,
cut the lemon into segments.
Make a parcel by layering two sheets of foil. Place all of the
vegetables inside the parcel, add the ginger, olive oil, port,
rosemary, bay leaf and lemon, season, seal tightly.
Cook over gentle heat for 15 minutes.

GRILLED FENNEL AND ZUCCHINI

Serves 6
Preparation time 15 minutes
Cooking time 10 minutes on the hotplate

3 young zucchinis
3 fennel bulbs
3 red onions
1 bird's eye chili
1 sprig rosemary
1 sprig fresh thyme
2 tablespoons soy sauce
2 tablespoons olive oil
salt and pepper

Slice the zucchini into thin strips, removing the seeds in the middle. Peel and slice the fennel bulbs and onions. Finely chop the chili, making sure you remove the seeds. Sear everything in the olive oil on the hot plate, add the thyme and rosemary, cook 10 minutes. Deglaze with the soy sauce, season.

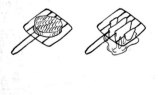

AGED COMTÉ BROCHETTES

Serves 6
Preparation time 30 minutes
Freezing time 15 minutes
Cooking time 5 minutes on the hot plate

7 oz aged Comté cheese (or gruyére)
⅓ cup sesame seeds
2 stale slices brioche
1 teaspoon sichuan peppercorns
2 eggs
½ cup olive oil
1 sprig fresh thyme

Cut the Comté cheese into ¾-inch cubes. Process together the sesame seeds, brioche and sichuan peppercorns. Whisk the eggs together with a fork. Dip the cubes of cheese in the beaten egg, then in the crumb mixture, place in the freezer for 15 minutes and repeat this process. Cook the cubes on the hot plate in olive oil on all sides until golden brown, skewer with a toothpick, serve with some tips of thyme.

CRUMBED MOZZARELLA

Serves 6
Preparation time 30 minutes
Freezing time 20 minutes
Cooking time 7 to 8 minutes on the hot plate

⅔ cup blanched pistachios
1 biscotte (slice of toasted bread)
1 teaspoon pepper
1 teaspoon dried thyme
3 balls of buffalo mozzarella
2 eggs
olive oil
sea salt

Process the pistachios with the biscotte, pepper and thyme. Take the balls of mozzarella out of their packaging and place them in the freezer for 15 minutes. Whisk the eggs together with a fork. Dip the mozzarella balls in the eggs then roll them in the pistachio crumbs, place them in the freezer for a further 5 minutes. Cook the mozzarella balls on the hot plate for 3–4 minutes then turn them over for a further 3–4 minutes. Place them in a small bowl, drizzle with a little olive oil and season with sea salt.

CAMEMBERT

With a cult figure

Serves 6
Preparation time 10 minutes
Freezing time 10 minutes
Cooking time 10 minutes over gentle heat

2 camemberts in wooden boxes (preferably
  from Normandy)
3 tablespoons calvados
herb assortment

Take the camemberts out of their wooden boxes. Soak the boxes in cold salted water for 10 minutes. Place the camemberts in the freezer for 10 minutes. Carefully cut a thin 'lid' off the top of the camembert, make incisions in the camemberts with a knife, sprinkle with calvados, scatter with herbs and replace the lid. Place the camemberts back into their boxes, wrap in foil and cook over gentle heat for 10 minutes.

Drink with: a red. Camembert has the ability to elevate the simplest red wine

ALMOND-CRUSTED GOAT'S CHEESE

Serves 6
Preparation time 10 minutes
Freezing time 15 minutes
Cooking time 5 minutes on the hot plate

6 firm goat's cheeses (preferably
  rocamadour cheeses)
1 cup flaked almonds
2 tablespoons liquid honey
1 tablespoon herbes de Provence (usually
  marjoram, oregano, rosemary, thyme)
coarsely ground black pepper
olive oil

Dip the cheeses in the honey, then in the flaked almonds,
making sure they stick well to the cheese. Sprinkle with
herbes de Provence and black pepper. Place in the freezer
for 15 minutes.
Sear the goat's cheeses, almond-side down, in the olive oil
on the hot plate for 2 minutes, turn them using a spatula
and finish cooking for 2 minutes on the other side.

PICODONS WITH ROSEMARY

With a cheese maker who's also rearing a pig

Serves 6
Preparation time 10 minutes
Cooking time 10 minutes over gentle heat, covered

18 very thin slices of speck (smoked ham or bacon)
6 matured goat's cheeses (preferably picodon cheeses)
6 sprigs rosemary

Arrange the slices of speck two by two in the shape of
a cross, place one cheese in the middle of each. Close up
like a wallet, hold in place with a sprig rosemary.
Cook over gentle heat 10 minutes, covered.

**Drink with: viognier with a subtle nose of apricot tart and
honey**

APPLES AND ROQUEFORT IN BRIK PASTRY

Serves 6
Preparation time 15 minutes
Cooking time 5 minutes on the hot plate

10½ oz roquefort cheese
2 granny smith apples
⅓ cup walnuts
1 egg
6 sheets of brik pastry (or filo pastry—see Note)
1 handful arugula
olive oil

Cut the roquefort cheese into thin slivers. Peel the apples,
halve them, remove the core and slice. Roughly chop the
walnuts. Lightly whisk the egg. Lay the roquefort cheese on
the sheets of brik pastry, scatter with walnuts, add the apples
and the arugula. Close to make a turnover, seal the edges with
egg. Cook the brik parcels on the hot plate in olive oil until
golden brown, 2–3 minutes each side.

Note: Brik is a Tunisian dish of pastry wrapped around food
and fried. Brik pastry is purchased in packages of rounds. It is
often called Malsouka and can be found in specialty food
stores. Filo pastry is an ideal substitute. Large Chinese round
wonton wrappers are also similar.

APPLES AND GINGER

With your intended, you need to make sure!!!

Serves 6
Preparation time 30 minutes
Cooking time 10 minutes on the hot plate

6 reine des reinettes apples (pippins)
juice of 2 lemons
2 tablespoons rum
3 tablespoons golden raisins
1 oz fresh ginger
⅓ stick lightly salted butter
3 tablespoons superfine sugar
3 tablespoons blanched pistachios
2 tablespoons blanched almonds

Peel the apples, remove the core, cut them into segments, sprinkle them with lemon juice.
Heat the rum with ½ cup water, add the raisins. Peel and cut the ginger into thin matchsticks.
Melt the butter on the hot plate, add the apples and the ginger, cook for 5 minutes. Add the sugar, drained sultanas (reserve the liquid), pistachios and almonds, cook for a further 5 minutes. Deglaze with the sultana water. Serve hot.

Drink with: vodka ginger cocktail, you need to forget!

BANANA FLAMBÉE

With the in-laws

Serves 6
Preparation time 5 minutes
Cooking time 10 minutes over gentle heat

1 vanilla bean
2 cups rum
6 ripe bananas
6 tablespoons sugar

The night before, split the vanilla bean in two and scrape out the seeds, and macerate the bean and seeds in the rum.
Place the bananas on the barbecue, cook 5 minutes on each side (the skin will blacken and start to split).
Heat ¾ cup of the vanilla rum on the barbecue, flambé.
On each plate, open up the banana skin, sprinkle with sugar and flambéd rum.

Drink with: the rest of the vanilla rum over 2 ice cubes

APPLE WITH ALMOND CREAM

With the children and their friends

Serves 6
Preparation time 20 minutes
Cooking time 15 minutes over gentle heat

⅓ cup ground almonds
2 tablespoons sugar
1 egg
6 granny smith apples
1 oz + 2¼ oz butter
2½ cups cider

Melt 1 oz butter, combine it with the ground almonds, sugar and egg. Put the whole mixture into a piping bag.
Peel the apples, core them whole, fill with the almond cream.
Make six foil parcels, divide the 2¼ oz butter between each one and the cider. Place an apple in each parcel and seal tightly, cook over gentle heat 15 minutes.

Drink with: the same cider, well chilled

MIRABELLE PLUM

With your nanna because she likes sweet things

Serves 6
Preparation time 10 minutes
Cooking time 15 minutes over gentle heat

1 lb 5 oz Mirabelle (small yellow) plums
2 cups muscat
3 tablespoons chestnut honey
2¼ oz butter
6 sprigs lemon thyme
1¼ cups heavy cream
¼ cup superfine sugar

Make six foil parcels and divide the plums between them.
Combine the muscat with the honey, sprinkle the plums
with this mixture, add some butter and lemon thyme. Seal
the parcels tightly, cook over gentle heat for 15 minutes.
Whip the cream to soft peaks, add the sugar. Open the
parcels, discard the lemon thyme, add a generous tablespoon
of chantilly cream. Serve immediately.

Drink with: round, rich and sweet muscat

FRUIT SKEWERS WITH COCONUT MILK POWDER

With Joséphine, Marie-Christine…

Serves 6
Preparation time 15 minutes
Cooking time 10 minutes over gentle heat

1 pineapple
2 mangoes
2 tablespoons rum
2 tablespoons honey
3 tablespoons coconut milk powder

Peel the pineapple, remove the 'eyes', cut into six segments
and remove the core. Cut the pineapple segments into slices
½ inch thick. Peel the mangoes, cut them into pieces
the same size as the slices of pineapple. Thread them onto
skewers, alternating pineapple and mango.
Combine the honey and rum, brush the skewers with this
mixture, sprinkle with coconut milk powder. Cook over
gentle heat for 10 minutes. The fruits should caramelize.

Drink with: Planter's Punch

APRICOT AND ROSEMARY SKEWERS

**With the neo-eco-bio-cool. We'll pick our own apricots,
cut some rosemary from the garden, a little organic
honey…**

Serves 6
Preparation time 15 minutes
Cooking time 5 minutes over high heat

18 apricots
12 stalks of rosemary
Orange syrup:
3 tablespoons honey
juice of 1 orange
1¾ oz lightly salted butter
½ cup peach liqueur

Cut the apricots in two, spear them on the stalks of rosemary,
making them overlap.
For the syrup, combine the honey with the orange juice,
reduce in a saucepan, add the butter and the peach liqueur,
reduce again: the texture should be syrupy.
Cook the apricot skewers over high heat for 5 minutes.
Serve immediately, coated with syrup.

**Drink with: non-vintage fizzy or a luscious sweet
chenin blanc**

APPENDICES

BL
OOP
ERS
& DIY BARBECUE

BARBECUE BLOOPERS

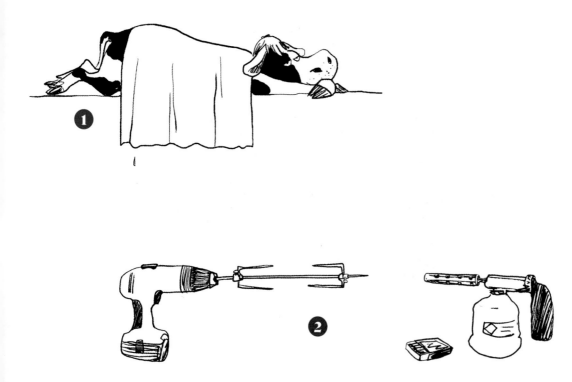

1- My wood isn't dry enough—free Turkish bath for
cow, calf and consort.
2- I get clever with the rotisserie—a fight breaks out.
3- I revive the barbecue with methylated spirits…
is something burning?
4- My coals are too hot, or the 'raw-burnt' diet.
5- I prepare a barbecue in midsummer in a high
wind, and replant a forest the following year.

Come and get
it while it's hot!

THE HIGH-TECH BARBECUE

1- The barbecutheque
2- UV lamp so you can still tan at night
3- Wood chopping block to keep grandpa happy
4- Carving board in case you have to share the beef rib cutlet...
5- Silver sauceboat from grandma's dinner service (have to keep her happy too)
6- Extinguisher...of thirst. That's funny, it's spraying rosé!
7- Supercar dashboard, turbo-charged (stainless steel design)
8- Barbecue FM set to "sausage.7 MHz"
9- Organic pantry, in case there's not enough meat
10- All-terrain 6 inch wheels

THE BARBECUE OF THE LONE FISHERMAN

THE INGREDIENTS:
a windproof firelighter
(it gets gusty by the
seaside)

dead leaves
(if they're not all gone
with the wind)

some twigs, nice and dry

some driftwood (keep the
best-looking piece to make
a lamp base)

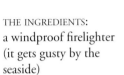

1 Dig a hole in the sand and
surround with rocks.

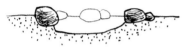

2 Place the dead leaves in the
bottom, without packing them
too tight.

3

4

Then arrange the twigs and
cross the pieces of driftwood
crossed. Make sure the air can
circulate.

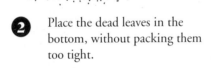

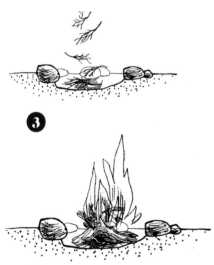

5 Light the dead leaves at the
bottom of the pile to make
a big flame

6 Let your wood burn until you get
some lovely embers.

If you haven't found anything
to make a barbecure grill, your
fishing rod will do the job.

Note: Be aware of fire restrictions
in all areas as well as restrictions
on the collection of firewood.

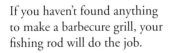

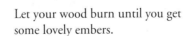

HOT PLATE BLOOPERS

1- I forgot to clean my hot plate, the beef will be doing its best sardine impression.

2- My hot plate isn't hot enough, it looks like a tableau of burned food.

3- Not having checked the gas level on Saturday, I have no choice but to improvize on Sunday.

4- I cook under a tree, it's guano sauce for lunch.

INDEX

INDEX BY RECIPE

INDEX BY MAJOR INGREDIENT

Heart
Chicken Heart Skewers 60
The Classic: Heart, Liver, Kidney 56

John Dory
John Dory 174

Lamb
Basil Lamb 50
Butterflied Lamb Shoulder 116
Emmanuel's Special Cutlets 148
Epigrams of Lamb with Tamarind 102
Garlic-Studded Lamb Leg Steak 116
Lamb, Cumin and Almonds 50
Massaman Lamb 50
Peppermint Lamb Leg Stead 116
Rack of Lamb with Tapenade 150
Saddle of Lamb 118
Spit-Roasted Lamb 164
Turkish Kebab 134

Liver
Peppered Calf's Liver 62
The Classic: Heart, Liver, Kidney 56

Lobster
Executed Lobster 190

Mackerel
Mackerel with Lemon 176

Mangoes
Fruit Skewers with Coconut Milk
Powder 242

Monkfish
Monkfish and Chorizo 66
Roast Monkfish 198
Rosemary-Skewered Monkfish 66

Mullet
Red Mullet Liver Toasts 180

Mushrooms
Grilled Cep Mushrooms to go
with a Good Piece of Meat 222
Onglet Kebabs 42
Veal and Ginger Skewers 54
Veal Sweetbread Skewers 60

Mussels
Éclade 208
The Ground-Dwellers 206

Oil
Basic Mayonnaise 22
Cocktail Mayonnaise 22

Garlic Mayonnaise 22
Garlic Mayonnaise 22
Herb Mayonnaise 22
Wholegrain Mustard Mayonnaise 22

Onions
Onions with Pepper Butter 214

Oysters
The Ground-Dwellers 206

Pineapple
Fruit Skewers with Coconut Milk
Powder 242
Pineapple Chicken Skewers 46

Plums
Mirabelle Plum 242

Pork
Andouillette en Papillote 126
Far West Ribs 144
Ham Burger 132
Honey Pork 34
Hot Dog 134
Pork Chop with Herbs 148
Pork Fillets with Pistachio Pesto 106
Pork Steaks & Wholegrain Mustard 148
Pork with Dried Fruit 34
Spit-Roasted Suckling Pig 162

Potatoes
Potatoes in Embers 212

Prawns
Beef and Prawns 38
King Prawns and Spring Vegetables 194
King Prawns with Fennel 190
Prawns Yakitori 74

Rabbit
Boned Saddle of Rabbit 104
Rabbit Thighs with Sundried
Tomatoes 102

Razor Clams
Razor Clams with Tarragon Butter 204
The Ground-Dwellers 206

Salt
Curry Salt 18
Provençal salt 18
Sichuan Salt 18
Spicy Salt 18

Salmon
Lemon Salmon 70
Olive-Basil Salmon 70

Roast Salmon 196
Salmon on Fir 200
Salmon Sauce Verte 186
Salmon Yakitori 74
Sesame Salmon 70

Sardines
Sardines 178

Scallops
Scallops and Speck 194
Scallops with Grilled Lettuce 194
Scallops Yakitori 74

Seabream
Black Seabream 172

Speck
Egg Burger 132
Picodons with Rosemary 234
Roast Monkfish 198
Sausage in the Embers 88
Scallops and Speck 194
Speck 122
Veal Fillet with Streaky Speck 34

Squid
Tarragon Squid 190

Tomatoes
Sauce Vierge 212
Spiced Tomatoes 212
Tomatoes with Lemon Thyme 218
Vegetables Grilled with Mint 222

Tuna
Shallot-Lime Yellowfin Tuna 186

Veal
Kidneys on Licorice 60
Like a Paupiette with Sweet Onions 108
Schnitzel and Aged Comté 122
Snail-Style Skewers 54
The Classic: Heart, Liver, Kidney 56
Veal and Ginger Skewers 54
Veal Chops with Shallot Butter 152
Veal Fillet with Streaky Speck 34
Veal Flank and Sarassou 122
Veal Roulade with Jamon 112
Veal Sweetbread Skewers 60
Veal Yakitori 76

Zucchini (Courgette)
Grilled Fennel and Zucchini 226

Text copyright © 2011 Murdoch Books Pty Ltd
Design copyright © 2011 Murdoch Books Pty Ltd
Photography copyright © 2011 Petrina Tinsley

Lyon Press is an imprint of Globe Pequot Press
Library of Congress Cataloging-in-Publication Data is available on file

ISBN 978-0-7627-7895-9

Photography: Marie-Pierre Morel
Illustrations: José Reis de Matos
Graphic design: Anne Martiréné
Copy-editing: Natacha Kotchetkova and Véronique Dussidour

English translation: Melissa McMahon
Editor: Carol Jacobson
Project editor: Laura Wilson
Production: Joan Beal

PRINTED IN CHINA

10 9 8 7 6 7 4 3 2 1